Begin S

Also in Right Way

Craft and Art – The Business
Improve Your Piano Playing
The Right Way to Read Music
The Right Way to Play Guitar
The Right Way to Draw
The Right Way to Draw People
The Right Way to Draw the Great Outdoors
Track Down Your Ancestors
The Independent Pensioner
Getting the Builders In
Paul Ripley's Expert Driving

Where to find *Right Way*

Elliot *Right Way* take pride in our editorial quality, accuracy and value-for-money. Booksellers everywhere can rapidly obtain any *Right Way* book for you. If you have been particularly pleased with any one title, do please mention this to your bookseller as personal recommendation helps us enormously.

Please send to the address on the back of the title page opposite, a stamped, self-addressed envelope if you would like a copy of our *free catalogue*. Alternatively, you may wish to browse through our extensive range of informative titles arranged by subject on the Internet at **www.right-way.co.uk**

We welcome views and suggestions from readers as well as from prospective authors; do please write to us or e-mail:
info@right-way.co.uk

Begin Sculpture

by

Ronald Unger

RIGHT WAY
plus

Typeset in 11/13½ pt Legacy Serif Book by Letterpart Ltd., Reigate, Surrey.

Printed and bound in Great Britain by Mackays of Chatham.

The *Right Way Plus* series is published by Elliot Right Way Books, Brighton Road, Lower Kingswood, Tadworth, Surrey, KT20 6TD, U.K. For information about our company and the other books we publish, visit our website at www.rightway.co.uk

Contents

Dedication

I would like to thank all the many people from all walks of life: artists, sculptors, musicians, teachers, scholars, farm hands, labourers, the old window cleaner – a marvellous man who had run for Britain in the 1924 Olympic Games – gentlemen, journeymen, vagrants and tramps who have helped me throughout my life and led up to my work as a sculptor and to the writing of this book.

Sadly, many of them are no longer with us but never have I forgotten them.

Regarding this book, I give a huge thank you to Malcolm Elliot for his patient and enduring editing and to the staff at Elliot Right Way Books for their help and support.

Thank you to my son Richard for his help with the graphics, photography and computer work, especially when things went wrong – as they too often did.

Grateful thanks as well to Michelle Dixon for the lovely poses, interest and encouragement.

Learn something every day as if you are going to live forever
Live every day as if it is going to be your last

Preface

This book is aimed at the beginner; that is, the person who has very little, or no, experience at all. In particular, I have in mind those who, for one reason or another, are unable to attend classes.

There is no substitute for good, practical instruction and help, and I am grateful to all those who, over the years, have given this to me. However, some people are compelled, or choose, to work alone. My aim in this book is that they should be able to do so starting virtually from scratch.

Some readers may find my early suggestions rather elementary but, I feel, I have no alternative. We either start from the beginning, assuming no knowledge or experience whatsoever, or we do not. With patience, perseverance and persistence, we can fairly quickly move on to more sophisticated work and, finally, to work of a high standard.

As far as this book is concerned, I had to make a decision where to stop. Since it is for beginners, I decided I would not include more advanced work or techniques. In modelling, I have gone as far as modelling a full-size head in clay, which is quite demanding. I have not included large figures which require complicated, internal, structural support or multi-piece moulds for casting. For carving, I have only used plaster because this is easy to acquire and work. I have not included other materials, such as wood, stone or metal because they require more expensive tools and equipment. Those readers who are fired with enthusiasm to work with them at a later stage will find plenty of help and assistance to do so.

Begin Sculpture, I hope, will enable your beginning. From here you should have laid the foundations for more advanced and demanding work, and a long and interesting experience.

No doubt this book will fall into the hands of experienced sculptors and teachers. I hope that they, too, may learn a few new tips from it.

Introduction

'Modelling and Sculpture' is an art form in three dimensions, unlike painting and drawing which are confined to only two dimensions.

Some people regard modelling and sculpture as two separate subjects and practise only one or the other but I regard both as branches of the same subject, 'sculpture'. Both branches are concerned with creating a work in three dimensions and both are subject to the same 'rules' or disciplines. Sculpture is mainly concerned with removing some of the original material: in stone, mostly by chipping, chiselling and grinding; in wood, by carving and sawing. Modelling is mainly concerned with adding and shaping material, although some of this may also be removed, cut, or carved. These differences are not strictly adhered to and often it is hard to distinguish how the work has been done.

What are the 'rules' or disciplines mentioned above? Unlike in painting, you cannot take colour into account. If you are painting the head of a girl with black hair, you paint it black but you cannot do this in sculpture. You only create the shape, or form, of the hair. You can see and paint the colours of the iris and pupil of the eyes but it is impossible to carve these colourings. This creates special problems which we will deal with when we come to them; it applies likewise to the lips, rosy cheeks and any other colourful parts of the body or subject. You are only concerned with the shape or form. I think it was Rodin, the great French sculptor, who said, 'Sculpture is about shapes and holes.' This should be a primary consideration throughout all your work. The drama, excitement, character and appeal of your work will largely depend upon your treatment of the 'shapes and holes', and how you arrange or design them. Other 'rules', such as construction and use of materials, will be considered as we proceed.

Many people feel inclined to take up modelling or sculpture but are put off by the cost of materials and tools, the work space required and because they think it is difficult. Often they turn to painting, usually in watercolour, because they think there are no such problems. Nothing could be further from the truth. A box of good watercolour paints will cost more than a large bag of clay. Watercolour brushes can be very expensive indeed – if they are any good – whereas the main tools you need for modelling and sculpture, your hands and fingers, are free. You need no more space to get started than you do for painting, i.e. a tabletop. As for difficulty, I think there is nothing more difficult than successful watercolour painting.

Of course, great sculptors work in many fine and expensive materials but this is a book for beginners and you must leave the fine materials until much later. We will use only the simplest and cheapest materials. However, don't be deterred by thinking these are only for the amateur. The best and finest sculptors of all time have all used the very same materials for countless centuries.

It seems fairly natural to want to create a masterpiece with your first effort but I must urge you not to be too ambitious to start with – though don't be too disappointed by this prospect. I have seen excellent work done by beginners on their first attempts. Always this success has been because they have kept the work simple and straightforward, stuck to the rules and not attempted anything too complicated.

I feel I should mention here the outstanding work done by many people living in so-called primitive cultures throughout the world. From the Arctic to Africa the carvings of the relatively untrained, indigenous peoples are some of the most exciting to be seen. Breathtaking in their simplicity and perception, I strongly recommend you to seek out pictures of this work – or, better still, find examples in galleries and museums. (However, do try to discriminate between the good and original, and the cheaper, mass-produced 'art', of which we see so much in gift and souvenir shops.) It is important that you should see as much work of others as you can – and not only that of the great and well-known masters.

At this stage it is as well to set out what we want to achieve:

1. Above all we want to have some fun. We can achieve this just by handling clay, running it through our fingers, banging it about, making little men or animals.

2. Next, we want to be creative. I think most people are creative and naturally artistic. Many will disagree with this but look at any baby child. Just as soon as he can hold a chalk he will start to draw houses, little men, animals and flowers, and quickly turn to sculpture – making charming little figures in Plasticine and dough.

3. We want a challenge. Again, this seems to be a natural instinct for most people. Some find the challenge in sport, in their work, in DIY projects. We are looking to art for our challenge. You will not be disappointed. Our challenge is both mental and physical.

4. We want excitement. You will be surprised how much excitement you will get in the execution of your work,

once you have overcome the preliminary stages. Your heart will pound, your nerves and courage will be tested; you will suffer mental and physical fatigue – with a glorious feeling of satisfaction.

5.　We want achievement. We want to feel we have done something worthwhile for no other reason than that we have done it and that it was worthwhile. Fame and fortune is not our purpose here, but you will have something to show for your effort that no other person has done. It is yours and yours alone; with care it will last forever, you can pass it on to your children and your children's children and they will all be proud of it – and of you.

It is not the purpose of this book to take into account commercial considerations. Some people seem to consider that the criterion for art that matters is whether or not you can sell it. I do not share this view. Of course it is flattering if someone wants to buy your work, but this should not be your objective – and surely not the prime criterion for the quality of your work.

For our purpose we will mainly use clay and Plasticine for modelling and plaster of Paris for carving. Many other materials can be used by the beginner, from soap and potatoes for carving to dough and wax for modelling but I think, at this stage, we should keep things simple and straightforward. Later you can experiment with other materials which may take your fancy, but it is important to grasp some of the basic principles first.

I propose to introduce two lesser known methods of producing three-dimensional work:

1.　Assemblage, or constructions. This form of sculpture has become increasingly popular over the last few decades, probably due to Picasso who used it to great effect. I am including it because not only can it be great fun but it is, perhaps, less demanding than conventional sculpture and very good results can easily be achieved.

2.   Carving – in plaster. Usually, plaster of Paris is used for making moulds and for casting work made from other materials but I am suggesting we use plaster as a medium 'in its own right' for creating original work. This is easy to execute, straightforward and enjoyable, and you can produce very good work.

You may find, especially if you have some previous knowledge, that some of the ideas in this book are rather unconventional. I include them, not for the sake of being different, but because I consider that some of the conventional methods, whilst quite sound, are cumbersome, difficult and unnecessary for the beginner. Wherever I stray from convention, I will give my reasons for doing so.

I have arranged the book in an order of development from the very first experience, progressing, step by step, to more ambitious work. The 'syllabus' is based on a course of instruction I occasionally give to beginners. Each chapter will be an advance on the previous work and gives suggested ideas. Technical and anatomical problems involved will be considered wherever necessary.

Readers are not required to stick rigidly to my suggestions regarding work and projects, or, necessarily, to progress from one chapter to the next in strict order. If you do not like my projects and have ideas of your own, please develop them. I would much prefer you to develop your own ideas than follow mine. My ultimate objective is that you should produce original work, not copies of other work.

If you want to skip a chapter or exercise, please do. One

thing, however, I must insist upon: *you must consider the rules and technical information given.* This is essential for all work; ignore them at your peril.

No matter what work you are doing you should always try to understand the material you are working with, its characteristics and constraints. If you are painting pictures, for example, you should make sure you understand the differences between oil paints, watercolours, pastels, acrylics and so on, and also the limitations and differences to be expected in the results. In general, it is a mistake to paint in one medium as if it were another; doing so loses the intrinsic beauty of each type. So it is with modelling and sculpture. Each material has distinct characteristics that should be exploited for the best, and most authentic, results.

Sometimes I am asked which materials I prefer – or find the easiest to work. I cannot answer this question because I enjoy them all. All have a character and beauty of their own which needs to be discovered. This, in itself, is a truly aesthetic and exciting experience. I find all are difficult. Wood because of the grain, which is never straight and can play merry tricks on you; marble because it can be brittle and have unexpected rifts which will crack just where and when you don't want them to; clay because it generally needs support and is difficult in fine areas; sheet metal because the work is slow and painstaking, requires a lot of 'elbow grease' to polish and often needs quite complicated welding techniques. Each offers its own unique challenge but, for now, I strongly recommend that you stick to the simple and easy materials.

If your ultimate aim is to produce good work you must be prepared to put in some hard graft. Don't be disappointed if you don't get good results quickly and easily. 'Genius', it has been said, 'is 90 per cent perspiration and 10 per cent inspiration.' Whilst few of us can aspire to genius, we must all be prepared to give the 90 per cent perspiration.

This does not mean that you are not going to have a good time and achieve satisfaction: quite the contrary, but much of the fun and satisfaction will come from overcoming the difficulties. In some ways it is a lonely life. You are alone with your work but, like walking alone in the rain across the fields, or being alone in a boat at sea, it is exciting. Paradoxically, you will not *feel* lonely. When you walk across the fields you develop a sense of communion with the countryside and weather. In a boat you and the sea become one, working together, mutually involved, achieving a common aim, pitting your strength against each other. So it is with sculpture. You must respect your material, your partner. If you do not, you will soon learn who is the master. I often feel I have a rapport with my work. It 'talks' to me, telling me what I can do and what I cannot. We develop a great respect for each other. My materials 'know' more about themselves than I do.

Chapter 1:

Down to Earth

When this well-known phrase first occurred to me as a chapter title I did not realise how appropriate it was. It is because the main material we shall use in this book for modelling is clay, and clay is, after all, earth. You cannot get much more basic than that. We are told that is where we come from and that is to where we shall return. Clay has been used by man for countless centuries for building, making bricks, lining wells, making artefacts and, perhaps finally, for producing art.

Clay is a lovely material because it is so malleable and tactile. To run clay through your fingers captures a glorious feeling; it is good for the skin, plentiful and cheap.

The clay which is most commonly used is a sedimentary material mainly composed of igneous rock and organic matter, deposited by rivers and other watercourses over the centuries. The deposits are compressed, as time passes, into a solidified mass and can be found almost everywhere.

As it is so widespread, some people like to collect their own but I do not recommend that to the beginner. Most of the collected clay will contain impurities and other materials which will have to be cleaned out before it can be used. It is much better to buy ready-prepared clay which has been thoroughly cleaned and 'wedged' – that is, manipulated into a dense, homogenous mass free from impurities, air pockets and excess moisture – and ready for modelling.

Modelling clay can be bought in small quantities from

most good art shops. To get started, you will need about 5 kilograms. As it is quite cheap, you must not be afraid to waste a fair amount. Large quantities can be purchased from specialist clay suppliers, whose names and addresses are given in the Appendix, but it is not worth buying large quantities if you are doing only limited work. Even though the clay is cheaper in bulk you usually have to pay the carriage unless you can collect it yourself. As the clay is so heavy, the carriage charge can be considerable.

Another great advantage of clay is that it keeps virtually forever. Unused and discarded clay can be stored in a strong plastic bag or plastic bin to prevent drying out – always squeeze out as much air as you can from a bag. If any clay does dry out completely, it can be recovered simply by soaking it in water – at the bottom of a bin or bowl. Cover it entirely with water about an inch (2.5cm) above the clay and be patient. If the water gets absorbed after a while, add more. After about a day it should be quite malleable and ready to work again. If it was very dry and hard, it may take longer and need more water.

Note that if your recovering clay is left too long it may become a soggy mess at the bottom. Should this happen, pour off as much water as you can – in a corner of the garden, not down the drain – and then leave it for the remaining water to evaporate until, once again, the clay is the right consistency. It should not then stick to your hands but needs to be damp enough to be malleable; as when purchased.

Some people tip a soggy mass, if they find themselves with one, onto an old cloth covered with newspapers to hasten the drying out. When working in small quantities this is hardly worthwhile and takes time. As the material is so cheap it is easier to buy some more so that you can get on with your work. However, if you are handling large quantities, it is economical.

There are a great many types of clay used for different purposes to achieve different results but, for the time being, do not get bogged down with this problem. All you need to buy is a good *modelling* clay. Most of this will be quite suitable but be sure it is *not* pottery clay which is differently formulated, especially for firing. Some dealers may sell a good 'all-round' clay which is suitable for both purposes but check before you buy. Most of the modelling clay sold is a reddish-brown but some is white or light grey. The general-purpose clay which I like to use is Potclays 1137 Standard Red. This is a very good, inexpensive clay intended for all-round use.

Clay is a fairly clean material. It can be a bit messy but I describe it as clean because it washes off clothes and cleans up easily. A lot depends on your own way of working. Whilst you are working with clay, if it is the right consistency, you should not find you make much mess or drop it about.

Working with Clay

It is worthwhile trying to 'work clean' and keeping things tidy and under control. Some people seem to like being in a mess but most professionals work very clean. You will find it is the easiest and quickest way of working. Some people have told me they are too lazy to keep things clean and tidy but I think *they miss the point*. Being neat and tidy is, actually, the laziest way of all as you do not have to waste time and energy clearing up, when you want to get on working. If you clean up your tools as you finish with them, you will find it easier and quicker than if you leave the clay to set dry on them. Keep a damp rag and some water nearby to wash your tools and hands in from time to time. (See also Working Methods in Chapter 4, page 48.)

Furthermore, if you don't keep your tools clean, you will find that bits and pieces of dry clay may interfere with your work, preventing a good finish and fine working.

The same applies to keeping tools reasonably tidy. Nothing is more irritating than being unable to find a tool when you want it. Of course, you can be too fussy but it is best to keep tools nearby, and in reasonable order, ready for working.

A light apron or an old shirt is good to work in and the dried clay marks will easily wash off. If you do get spatter marks on the hard surfaces of nearby furniture they will wipe off with a damp rag. Carpets or upholstery need a little more attention. Wipe the clay off as soon as possible with damp rags or a car sponge with, perhaps, a little detergent, and you should have no problem remaining.

Obviously, a good working space is preferred. In the summer you can work in the garden but be careful the clay does not dry out too quickly in the heat and sun. In the winter you may be forced to work undercover in the kitchen, garage, conservatory or an outhouse. It is very useful if you have a working space where the work can be left in between working times, rather than have to restore the space to its everyday use. This is not always possible but an outhouse or shed can usually be found. I have often had to work in them and if necessary, when it is very cold, I use an electric heater.

Materials

Clay cannot be beaten as a modelling material, not only because it is so malleable but also, whilst it remains so, because it can be added to or removed from your work. This allows for changes to be made quite easily to your original idea and also to correct any errors you may make. I'm afraid this facility will be denied you when carving.

Among the disadvantages of clay, one is that it has a low structural strength. Structurally, it has very little ability to stand up on its own and, generally, it needs supporting.

Small figures may stand quite well without support. This depends on the clay and the amount of moisture but most standing figures need some sort of structural support. For small or simple figures, a single, central column is sufficient. More complicated and large figures require an internal framework called an *armature* which can be likened to the skeleton of your body. However, these fall beyond the scope of this book.

The next disadvantage is that clay is not very durable. Generally, the finished work is not likely to last very long or very well. Once dried out it will become brittle and parts may break off. Furthermore, as it dries out, you may find that some nasty cracks occur. To some extent this depends on the quality of your work, the outside humidity and the temperature but you must always be prepared for it. Therefore, if you want to preserve your work you will need a simple but effective way of doing so.

The most common way of preserving sculptures modelled in clay is to cast the finished figure in another material – such as plaster. Resins or metals, like bronze, are also used but are not really for the beginner. Casting in plaster is very satisfactory and can be done at home. You need to make the moulds for this purpose whilst your clay remains moist. However, all the detailed technique will be considered later, in Chapter 4.

Potters render their work permanent by firing it in a kiln. This can be done with clay sculptures but requires a kiln and knowledge of kiln work. *The preliminary exercises you will find in Chapter 3 really need to be fired if you want to keep them.* In this case a local art school or friendly potter may help you out.

Plasticine is also a good material to work with. It is more expensive than clay but can be justified for small figures. There are several varieties available all with similar characteristics. Its great advantages are that it does not dry out or crack quickly and it remains fairly permanent when finished. On the other hand, as it never gets hard, it can easily get dented, bent or distorted. Whilst Plasticine is cleaner to work with than clay, it does not clean off surfaces or clothes so easily. I don't like it as much as clay as it is not so malleable and you can't work as much with your hands.

I love working clay with my hands. I think they are the best and most enjoyable tool of all. Plasticine is rather different in this respect and mainly has to be worked with modelling tools. However, I do use it frequently for small figures, where its 'stiffness' is a help with detail. It is also a great advantage if you want to work over a longer period of time for it can be left much longer without drying out appreciably, and you don't have to worry about keeping it moist. Quite a few well-known sculptors use it for this reason. (However, it does go dry after several months so keep it as airtight as you can and in a warm place.)

Some sculptors and commercial houses use wax for modelling. I do not recommend this for a beginner. It is difficult to buy locally, and using it requires experience and special metal tools. I mention it as you may wonder how some results that you see in shops and galleries are achieved. Later, you may want to experiment with wax but you will have to get it from specialist suppliers.

Whilst I do not wish to depart from my recommendation that a good modelling or all-purpose clay will be quite suitable for your work, I feel I should mention a couple of other special clays. Although they are not so easy to come by and have to be purchased from specialist dealers, they do have qualities which are very good and useful. Their main advantages are that, used carefully, they are less likely to crack or crumble as they dry out, and they solidify into a very satisfactory, permanent figure. This is very useful if you only want one figure and do not want to mould and cast that figure into another medium.

The two clays are:

1. Potclays 1114 Craft Crank.
2. Potclays 1150 Modelling Clay.

These two clays differ quite considerably but are both delightful to work with.

Potclays 1114 Craft Crank is a 'buff/toast' coloured, coarse modelling clay with plenty of 'grog' in it. 'Grog' is fired clay ground into small pieces. The grog is carefully sifted for size and thoroughly wedged into the base clay, giving a very interesting texture. I like this clay very much and strongly recommend it – as the coarse texture compels you to work without finicky detail. It shrinks very little and is ideal for larger figures and full-size portraits. Colour can be successfully added to the dried and finished figure giving a wholly delightful effect. (Figs. 31 and 46 were done in this clay.)

Potclays 1150 Modelling Clay is a very finely ground, off-white, clay, this one being quite suitable for detailed work and which, again, will harden without cracking or crumbling. I have used both these clays quite often and found they will withstand the minor bumps and the ravages of time extremely well. (Fig. 43 was done with this 1150 Modelling clay.)

I do not always colour these clays because I like their natural finishes. This is a matter for personal taste and the suitability of the subject.

Chapter 2:

Getting Started

Working Space, Tools and Equipment

Working Space

I doubt if many readers will have a permanent space in which to work. Fortunately, you do not need very much. You need very little equipment either, and few tools. It is not necessary to buy a special modelling stand at this stage. The kitchen table or a bench in the garage will do fine. If you are working on your kitchen table, I recommend you cover it with a plastic tablecloth – the vinyl type with linen backing is best; a polythene sheet is not very satisfactory for this purpose because it, and everything on it, tends to slide about. This may not be necessary if the table has an impervious top from which you can easily clean off any mess. You will also need a smaller piece, about 18 inches (45cm) square of similar, plastic/vinyl material on which to roll out clay. Many potters and sculptors use hessian for this purpose but I prefer vinyl as it has no hairs.

Other Equipment

You will also need a working surface or board. Chipboard with a hard white surface is excellent as it cleans off easily. I always use this to work on. The thicker the board, the better it is for this purpose. It is a very good idea to screw two equal-thickness battens across the underside of the board, parallel and about 1½ inches (3.75cm) in from each of two opposite edges. This will not only prevent it from warping but make it much easier to lift when you want to move it.

The size of the board depends on the size of the figure you are making. For my small maquettes (see Chapter 6), which are about 9 x 4 inches (23 x 10cm), a board of, say, 12 x 8 inches (30 x 20cm) would be sufficient and battens are not necessary. For a larger, reclining figure you need a board at least 6 inches (15cm) larger all round than the figure. (Often, I find the size of such figures is actually determined by the size of the board I happen to have available!) For a full-size head you need a board not less than 15 inches (38cm) square. Battens are essential here because the finished head is quite heavy and difficult to lift and move. However, for general purposes, and if you do not want too many sizes of board lying around, a board of about 18 inches (45cm) square will suit most small pieces.

You will probably need something to protect your clothes; as suggested earlier, an apron or an old shirt will be fine.

A simple turntable is not essential but very useful. It is the only special piece of equipment I strongly recommend. The advantages of a turntable, especially when you are working at home, are that you can easily work all sides of the figure without getting up, walking round the table, stretching across the work or trying to rotate your work-board itself. It also raises the work from the table, which gives you much more freedom of movement for your hands and arms.

There is no need to buy an expensive professional model. There are several inexpensive ideas which provide quite satisfactory solutions. For example, some time ago, when I was on holiday, I was asked to do a head for the family I was staying with. I had no equipment or tools. I bought a bag of clay and some cheap, plastic modelling tools from a nearby

Fig. 1(a). Inexpensive plastic modelling tools.

art shop and a plastic revolving stand, normally used for icing cakes, from a cookery shop. This I found to be excellent and I still use it. Old, rotating, marble cheese boards are very useful, if you can find one. DIY enthusiasts can make an excellent turntable by using the 'Lazy Susan' device, which can be purchased from craft and woodworking shops.

To sum up, you need:

A modestly sized table or bench.

A vinyl tablecloth with a linen backing – if necessary to protect the table you are working on. A work sheet of similar material, about 18 inches (45cm) square, for rolling out the clay.

A sturdy, smooth, hard-surfaced work-board, about 18 inches (45cm) square with two parallel battens screwed underneath.

An inexpensive turntable – not essential but recommended.

A protective apron or an old shirt.

Tools

The best tool for working clay is the hand. I think about 90 per cent of my clay work is done by hand but some of the following will be useful:

A set of cheap modelling tools (see Fig. 1(a)). For larger work, more substantial, looped modelling tools are very useful for removing large amounts of clay (see Fig. 1(b)). Other examples and some wooden ones are shown in Figs. 1(c) and 1(d). A selection of these should be all you need. A miniature trowel can also be handy.

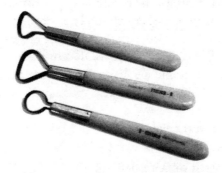

Fig. 1(b). Looped modelling tools for removing large amounts of clay.

For cutting out templates (see Chapter 3) a Stanley knife and a steel rule are recommended.

An old table knife, a small kitchen knife, even a spoon and fork have their uses.

A wooden meat or barbecue skewer.

A pencil with a rounded top. (This is not for drawing but will come in useful for modelling.)

Two, matching, straight strips of wood which need to be about 12 inches (30cm) long, 1 inch (2.5cm) wide and about three-eighths of an inch (1cm) thick – and a quite large, wooden rolling pin. I prefer one without handles. A little cooking oil to rub onto your rolling pin will prevent the clay from sticking to it. These items are used when rolling out slabs of clay.

Fig. 1(c). Wooden modelling tools.

Toothpicks and matches are useful. Make sure the matches are the old-fashioned, brown-headed safety matches as the red-headed ones tend to disintegrate if they get damp.

A length of piano wire, used like a cheese cutter, for cutting the clay – or a special clay cutter – is almost essential but not expensive. Clay cutters are made from stainless steel wire which is a great advantage. If you buy one of these – sold by craft shops – the ends will be attached to dowel sticks but, if you use piano wire, you will have to attach the ends to dowel sticks of your own, so as to prevent cutting your hands.

As mentioned in Chapter 1, keep some water, old rags – old shirts and tea towels are the best – and a car sponge handy for cleaning up. A cheap, plastic, flower-spray enables you to refresh your work and to keep it moist as you are working.

Later, you will need some callipers for the face and head but don't buy an expensive pair to start with. You can make perfectly good callipers yourself. Instructions and an illustration are given in Chapter 8.

Initially, it is not necessary to set yourself up with all the equipment I have listed. They are just suggestions which you might find helpful to start with and to which you can add as you proceed. It is better to add to your collection as you progress and have a clearer idea of your needs.

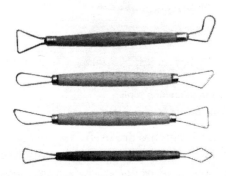

Fig. 1(d). Wire modelling tools.

Perhaps a word about the price and quality of professional tools and equipment might be helpful here. I have emphasised that you should only use inexpensive tools to begin with and adapt wherever you can. My cake-stand turntable cost less than £20 whereas a professional turntable will cost over £100. However, a professional model is much more robust, will not rust or warp with moisture or heat, is much more firm and rigid and will last much longer.

The same applies to modelling stands upon which to

work as opposed to standing or sitting at a table or bench. Professional modelling stands are essential for the professional sculptor but not necessary for the beginner. If you feel the need to have a stand which is apart from your table and which can be moved easily or rotated as you work, I have found that a kitchen stool with a threaded central support is quite adequate, and entirely suitable for when you are sitting down. (See Fig. 2.)

Fig. 2. Adjustable height kitchen stool.

It is the same with modelling tools. Professional tools, for example those made of carefully selected boxwood, are lovely to handle and work with but are expensive. You can get started with the cheaper plastic tools and treat yourself, occasionally, to more expensive tools as you go along. This will help you avoid extravagant and unnecessary purchases. Modelling tools are not standardised in design or in size. Every manufacturer, worldwide, produces its own range; so look out for those tools which will suit you the best. I have tools which I have collected over time but never use as I never seem to need them. On the other hand, I have some 'favourites' which I use often – including the round-topped pencil and the safety matches! There are also some very good stainless steel tools available but they, too, are expensive. Keep your eyes open for bargains. Some of the best tools I have were also the cheapest and bought in open-air markets both in England and abroad.

Chapter 3:

Preliminary Work with Clay

Many people want to do something exciting and then straightaway have something to show for their efforts. If you feel you want to make more rapid progress, you can skip this chapter and move on. However, I think that some preliminary working with clay is worthwhile – especially if you are not familiar with its texture and characteristics. The following suggestions are rather like the 'Five Finger Exercises' beginners play when learning the piano; they are not meant for display but for practice.

I must re-emphasise that these are preliminary exercises in clay and are NOT SUITABLE FOR KEEPING UNLESS THEY ARE FIRED. If you want to have your work fired to keep, I am sure you will find a friendly potter with a kiln or, as suggested earlier, possibly a local art school may help you.

Perhaps this is my first departure from the conventional approach for, whilst this book is not about pottery and ceramics, I suggest that similar work is where we start. For these exercises – and later work – you will need your workboard, the two strips of wood listed in Chapter 2, the rolling pin, the piano wire or clay cutter and the vinyl 'work sheet' – on which to roll out clay.

First, take a good handful of the clay. (Be sure to re-wrap the remaining clay to prevent it drying out.) Toss this around in your hands for a while. Take note of the texture and feel. If the texture is just right, as it should be when you buy it, you will find it is nicely malleable without sticking to your hands. Should it be at all sticky, it may be helpful to rub a very little cooking oil into your hands. If you have to use your piano wire to release the clay from the board at any time, make sure it is quite taut.

As you work clay, it may begin to dry out a little. If it dries out too much, whilst working, add a little water with the flower-spray – but not too much – a little at a time is better than too much.

With larger amounts it is a good idea, before you start working with it, to bang the clay down onto your work-board and lift it again, several times. This helps eliminate any hidden pockets of air.

Pinch Pots

I suggest, as a start, making a 'pinch pot'. Some of you may have made these at school. Make a ball of clay, which fits into the palm of one hand. (It should be larger than a golf ball but smaller than a tennis ball.) Next, press the thumb of your other hand in, towards the centre of the ball. Now comes the tricky bit. Rotate the ball of clay, little by little, whilst continuing to press that thumb a little more into the centre each time the ball is rotated, at the same time spreading the clay outwards. Press, rotate and spread; press, rotate and spread. (See Fig. 3.) Don't let the pot wall or the bottom get too thin; both need to remain quite firm. Keep on until you have a good-shaped little pot or bowl. After some practice you can do this with a smooth action, producing a nice round pot. If you drop it carefully onto your work-board, this will make a flat bottom for it to stand on. (In olden days, that was how pork pies were shaped.)

Coil Pots

Now try making a coil pot. This is a little more difficult. First make a long 'string' of clay, about a quarter of an inch

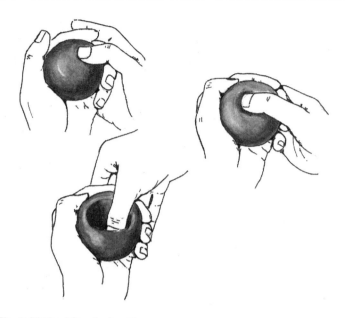

Fig. 3. Method for pinch pots.

(0.5cm) thick, by rolling it out, evenly, by hand on the reverse side of your work sheet[1]. Hold this 'string' of clay at one end, very carefully so that it will not break, and, starting in the centre, wind the coil around until you have a small circle, say about 3 inches (7.5cm) in diameter. When you have made this first 'circle', make another *on top of the outer ring only*, and then another – on top of that – then another and another until you have a good-sized pot. (See Fig. 4.) If necessary, make another string of clay to continue. Make sure they are firmly joined together but without distorting the shape of the string or pot. Each layer should be pressed

---

[1] You use the reverse side of the work sheet for rolling out your clay to make the string because this helps prevent the clay from sticking – as it would tend to do on the smooth side. However, the smooth side can be used on other occasions, such as during modelling, when it can be easily cleaned up afterwards.

fairly firmly against the one below. If necessary add just a suggestion of water between the layers. This is a very ancient technique, and quite large and beautiful pots can be made this way. Even the most experienced potters regard this method as a challenge.

Fig. 4. Method for coil pots.

Slab Work

'Slab Work' is another ancient technique still used widely today throughout the world and one which can produce the most marvellous results. As the name implies, the work is made from slabs of clay; so, first, we must make the slabs. This is quite easy. First, you roll out some clay as explained below. Again, so that it will lift off easily, do this on the *reverse* side of the vinyl work sheet. Rub a little cooking oil onto your rolling pin, as well, to help prevent it sticking. I suggest you work like this: take your two identical strips of wood and place them on the work sheet, apart and parallel. The distance apart is not important but it must be less than the length of your rolling pin. Roughly fill the gap between the wood strips with clay and start by knocking it down with the side of a clenched fist. Next take your rolling pin and carefully roll the clay down to the thickness of the strips of wood, removing any surplus clay or filling in where necessary until you have a good even surface. (See Fig. 5.)

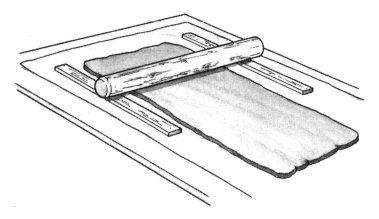

Fig. 5. Rolling clay.

You can now cut shapes out of the slab you have made and form them into various works. The simplest is a tile. For this cut a 6 inch (15cm) square template out of stiff cardboard – using the steel rule and the Stanley knife. Don't do this on your work sheet or you will cut it. Place a piece of thick cardboard or MDF (medium-density fibreboard) between the two first.

Place the template on your clay and cut carefully round it with your *kitchen knife*. Do not use the Stanley knife or, again, you may cut through your work sheet below. Let your tile dry out a little. When it is 'leather hard' – a little more than half-dry – you can inscribe some motif or hieroglyphics into the surface with a modelling tool or penknife. You can also add little squat legs to the corners of the reverse side: cut out small squares from the rolled out clay and use 'scratch and dab' to attach them to the tile. This means that you first lightly score the surfaces to be joined and dampen them a little with water. Then you press them together reasonably firmly and leave it all to dry.

Usually tiles are glazed but unglazed tiles can be very attractive and useful. This tile might well make a plant or teapot stand but it will need to be fired if you want to keep it and use it for this purpose. Your friendly potter should be able to advise you on glazing.

Another idea for a tile is to make a shallow dish from it. Cut a tile as you did the first one but smaller, say about 4 inches (10cm) square. Place this carefully on the top of a smooth plastic ball and gently press down all round to make a concave dish. The size of the ball is not important – the larger the ball, the shallower the dish. If you rub a tiny amount of cooking oil on the surface of the ball it will help when you come to release it.

Leave that where it is.

Now make a short cylinder to become your dish stand, about 1 inch (2.5cm) deep and as wide as your eye 'fancies' but not too wide. Do this as described below under **Cylindrical Pots**. Then attach this, centred underneath the exposed side of the tile, with 'scratch and dab'. Invert the whole, carefully, and let the dish, on its stand, drop into your hand. You should have a very nice aperitif dish. (See Fig. 6.)

These little dishes are very attractive if they are made with rough clay (Potclays 1114) which contains plenty of grog (see page 23), fired, and then glazed. It is pleasing to use a blue or green glaze, which you mostly wipe off with an old

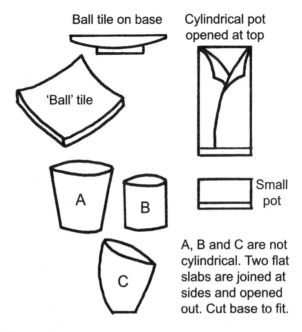

Ball tile on base

Cylindrical pot opened at top

'Ball' tile

A

B

Small pot

C

A, B and C are not cylindrical. Two flat slabs are joined at sides and opened out. Cut base to fit.

Fig. 6. Slab work.

rag or sponge so that the glaze remains in the little cavities. (Talk to your potter about this technique.)

You can also make some 'stylised' wall plaques from slab clay, for example of fish. From a slab of clay first cut out a characterised outline. Then score some indented lines to divide the surface into areas to suit the design. Pressing the edge of a plastic ruler, or similar item, into the surface will do this. Then, break up the surface of some of these areas with various patterns: triangles, rounds, points and so on. Use your imagination and find implements which you can use for this purpose. A pencil will be very handy. You can use the round or hexagonal end for some sections; and the pointed end, laid at an angle, will produce an interesting effect like fish scales. Other ideas for wall plaques may occur to you. There are no rules; just experiment, and aim for originality.

Bonsai Pots

A very attractive Bonsai pot can quite easily be made from slabs. You need to cut a bottom, two side pieces and two end pieces. These need to be fairly accurate so it is best to make templates. An example is given in Fig. 7. First, cut out your base from rolled out clay, and set it aside. Then cut out a side and an end. These are placed at right angles to each other on top of the base. Assuming you will want to have your pot fired and keep it, you must make the joints strong by using 'scratch and dab', as described earlier in this chapter. Now assemble the opposite walls and corner and treat the same way. Be sure all joints are scored and dampened before fitting them together, so that they will dry out really secure. You should now have a fairly rigid little box, which can already be handled with care. Allow it to dry out slowly and, whilst still 'leather hard', inscribe the sides with the point of a knife or other tool if you wish.

You can also, using the same techniques, make a tray for your pot to stand on. Make this tray about an inch (2.5cm) both longer and wider than the pot, and with sides only about half an inch (1.25cm) high. You can put a little cube at each corner for feet – which makes it very attractive – but be sure to attach them properly with 'scratch and dab'. Allow the whole thing to dry out completely before having it fired. Your bonsai pot in its tray will look most attractive.

Cylindrical Pots

It is not difficult to make cylindrical pots from slabs of clay. For a small pot, you need the same thickness of clay as we have used above (i.e. the thickness of your two strips of

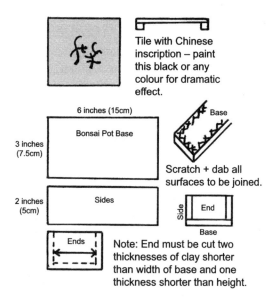

Fig. 7. Bonsai pot.

wood – see page 28 and Fig. 5). After the clay is rolled out, remove the wood strips and cut the ends square so that you now have a rectangle of clay. Its width needs to be about the height you want your cylinder to be, and its length should be at least equal to the circumference of your rolling pin, with about half an inch (1.25cm) extra for overlap. Roll the clay, lengthways, around your rolling pin after lightly moistening the latter with cooking oil. Allow the clay to overlap a little and 'scratch and dab' before pressing down to make a firm joint. Cut off any surplus overlap out of your way. Make another small slab of clay for the base, just larger than your cylinder is round, and 'scratch and dab' the top surface. Slip the cylinder of clay to one end of your rolling pin (carefully rotate the rolling pin, if necessary). Hold the cylinder, still with the rolling pin inside, a little above the base slab you have just made. Now lower both on to the slab. With the rolling pin still inside for support, attach the clay wall securely to the base. Cut off surplus base clay around the outside edge. Now remove the rolling pin and you will have a neat, free-standing flowerpot. If you want to enhance it further, you can spread out the join at the top as shown in Fig. 6. When dry, this could be fired.

Fig. 8. Method for larger cylindrical pots.

Larger pots can be made the same way by using a cardboard tube – the sort used when buying prints – or a length of plastic pipe. In this case you may need a thicker clay wall. (Some potters have several thicknesses of paired-up wood strips ready for this purpose.) Before applying the clay, cover the tube with newspaper (see Fig. 8). The clay will then slip off easily.

More examples of slab pots are given in Fig. 6.

With all this work, make sure the sections will become firmly attached together when dry, by using 'scratch and dab'. After gently pressing the clay together to make a strong weld, smooth the joins by running a damp modelling tool, finger or the end of a spoon along them.

Slab Sculpture

Charming little animal figures can be made from slab clay as seen in Fig. 9(a). Make these figures not less than 4 inches (10cm) long for the bear and tall for the squirrel. Take the bear. Cut out a profile as shown in Fig. 9(b) from a slab of clay. (Start, as before, with a cardboard template.) Then fold this slab profile over a suitable cylinder to form the bear. If you do not have a suitable cylinder, roll one out of clay, tapering it towards the head. You can add/shape the ears and tail, and, so that it will stand up, form stubby feet.

Fig. 9(a). Small animal figures.

With the squirrel, cut *two* matching profiles from your slab of clay. Stand a tapered cone of clay on end and shape these two 'halves' of the body around this. Leave the arms

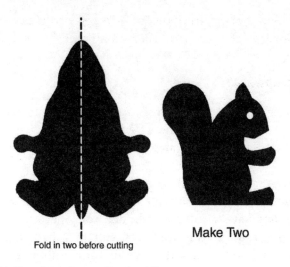

Fold in two before cutting

Make Two

Fig. 9(b). Templates for small animal figures.

and legs apart. Do not join the head. You will notice that the front of the head has a roughly triangular piece wedged between the sides to give it extra shape. Cut this shape in some slab, to match your figure, and then fix it in place with 'scratch and dab'. Then, join the tails together with 'scratch and dab'.

Simple human figures can be made from strips of clay cut from a slab, as shown in Figs. 10(a) and 10(b). These little manikins are great fun and challenge the imagination. They also provide good experience in getting used to proportions and action poses. Making some of your own gives you really worthwhile early practice.

Having worked through these exercises, I hope you will continue with this work, developing your own ideas.

Fig. 10(a). Practice manikin.

Fig. 10(b). More manikins.

Chapter 4:

Making Moulds and Casts – An Introduction

Most students will want to preserve a good deal of their work and the easiest way to do this is by making plaster casts. However, if you are not careful, much of your work will turn out to be unsuitable for casting; whereas, with a little preliminary instruction, thought and care, the same work may be made quite suitable.

I have gone into the subject at some length, at this stage, because I feel it will stand you in good stead and be a useful reference for all your future work.

First I should mention that the figure you make, whatever the material, is always known as the 'original'. Then you make a mould of this original by covering it with plaster. This mould is called the 'negative' or 'female'. When the mould is set quite hard and dry, it is separated from the original and filled with casting plaster. This cast, when subsequently released, becomes your final piece of sculpture and is called the 'positive' or 'male'.

It is important with clay figures like those described in this book that you carry out the moulding stage whilst the clay is still quite moist and no more than about half dry.

Before you start you will need to obtain plaster and some suitable release agents. These are used to coat the inside of a mould before casting, so that, when the cast is dry, the mould will come away freely.

PLASTER

Plaster of Paris or, simply, plaster, is a rigid, inflexible, durable substance when set. That is why it is used so successfully in setting fractured bones. You cannot bend, stretch or manipulate it once set. There are a great many plasters on the market, stocked in your builder's merchants for building purposes, but they are all unsuitable.

YOU MUST HAVE CASTING PLASTER.

Casting plaster – the specific product you need – is used throughout for making both the mould and the cast.

It is unlikely that your local builder's merchants will have this in stock but they will usually order a sack or two for you. However, although this is the cheapest way of buying it, the quantity may be more than you need and can usefully store. (It does deteriorate with time.) In this case you can buy smaller quantities from your local chemists' shops. They always seem to have a bag or two in stock – ready for a broken arm. It is of excellent quality and quite cheap. It is the best way of buying it for the person who is not going to need large quantities.

Plaster is thermoplastic. As it transforms from a liquid to a solid, a chemical action takes place and it heats up. Put the palm of your hand gently on a freshly made mould and you will feel that it is quite warm. It is not fully set until cold. It is best to leave it a little longer to 'cure' completely. I usually leave plaster at least 24 hours to cure, by which time it will be quite hard and durable. If you are anxious to get on, you can use a mould once it has set cold but handle it with care as it still contains some moisture and may break more readily.

Mixing Plaster for your Moulds

It is best not to mix too much plaster, only enough for the job in hand with a little to spare. For larger figures it is best to make two or three mixes rather than trying to cover the whole figure in one application. For this work I usually mix the casting plaster in a plastic washing-up bowl but for smaller jobs a smaller bowl will do. Half fill the bowl with clean water. Take a handful of plaster and sprinkle it on to the water, carefully spreading it around, adding more until one or two peaks are showing; then begin to stir *quite gently*. (Make sure not to introduce air if it can be avoided.) A long wooden spoon is ideal for this. You must remove all lumps. Lumps will prove to be disastrous. Usually, you have to get your hands in and rub the mix between your fingers until you cannot feel any lumps. If your hands are sensitive to plaster use latex rubber gloves, which are quite cheap.

It is difficult to describe the best consistency for the mix; this depends upon the application and is largely a matter of trial and error. However, here are three Mixes which, as a general guide, meet most moulding requirements:

1. *Thin*. Mix 1 is about the consistency of full cream milk. Used for flicking on to vertical subjects and for the first coat of a waste (or single use) mould. Mix the plaster into the water until creamy but still quite runny. Very thin and brittle when set. (10 parts plaster to 8 parts water by weight.)

2. *Medium*. (Most used.) Mix 2 wants to be about the consistency of a thick double cream, offers a little resistance to the spoon as you mix but runs off freely. It can be poured, will not spread out much and sets soon after pouring. Use this for most of your mould making and for reinforcing the first coat of either a waste or a vertical mould. (Both of these are explained later in this chapter.) When fully set it is quite tough. (10 parts plaster, 7 parts water.)

3. *Thick.* Mix 3 is quite firm, just drops off the end of the mixing spoon, and sets quickly. Just before it sets, you can spread and manipulate it into position. Used for building up extra reinforcements and – later in your experience – for making figures directly in plaster. The latter technique, however, is beyond our scope in this book. (10 parts plaster, 5 parts water.)

Note that Mix 2 becomes Mix 3 after a short while and that, the thicker the mix, the quicker it sets *and* the stronger it is.

When you have the correct mixture you can apply it to your figure to make your mould. As will be explained, this can be done by pouring for horizontal figures, by flicking for vertical work or, when the occasion suits, by applying the thicker mixture by hand or with a miniature trowel.

Essentially, there are four types of moulds:

1. One piece moulds.

2. Waste moulds.

3. Two piece moulds.

4. Multiple moulds.

In this book we will only consider the first three of these as multiple moulds fall outside the scope of the beginner. However, before we do so, there are one or two preliminary considerations to be taken into account.

Working Methods

An important further word is needed, here, before we move on. IT IS ESSENTIAL THAT YOU DO NOT WASH YOUR

HANDS, EQUIPMENT, TOOLS OR MATERIALS IN A
SINK OR UNDER A TAP WHICH RUNS INTO A SINK OR
DRAIN. The last thing you want is to have your sink
blocked with plaster – or even clay, for that matter.

You can buy, or make, special sink traps for this purpose
but they are not necessary for the beginner so long as he
proceeds with care. I find it quite easy to work with a
large, rectangular, plastic, storage box which I keep nearby
– half filled with water – for all cleaning up. All the mess,
plaster (or clay) is thus contained within and will sink to
the bottom. I clean my tools in this box. As soon as I have
finished using a tool I throw it into the box. Any material
clinging to it just falls off and the rest keeps quite soft
ready to be wiped off with an old rag. Frequently, I rinse
my hands in it. From time to time and at the end of the
day, I remove all the tools and clean and dry them with an
old rag. Do not allow wooden tools to remain in the water
for too long. When you finish for the day, pour off the
surplus water – on the garden – and scrape out all the
sludge from the bottom. If you are lucky you may have a
corner of garden, behind a shrub or somewhere, where this
can be dumped. If not, tip it onto several layers of newspaper, let it dry out a bit – overnight if possible – then
wrap it up and put it in a plastic bag ready for taking to
the rubbish tip. Give your bowl a good rinse ready for the
next time.

Undercuts

An UNDERCUT is a part of the original which is over-
hanged by another part and therefore prevents the original,
or a cast, from being removed from the mould without
damage. An example is the nose. If plaster were to enter one
of the nostril cavities whilst making the mould, it would be
impossible to remove the mould without breaking it off or

breaking that side of the nose. This is a rather dramatic example but more gentle undercuts occur frequently and, whenever possible, are best prevented.

Another example can be examined by considering a cooked sausage. In the unlikely event that we wanted to make a mould of a sausage, we might first assume that the thing to do would be to encase the whole sausage in plaster. However, it would then seem impossible to remove the sausage without breaking that plaster – which is true! Nonetheless, sometimes this breaking away of the plaster is done – but this will be from the final cast, rather than the original. *Because this mould is broken away from the final cast it can never be used again.* It is thus *wasted* and therefore called a WASTE MOULD.

If you look along the whole length of a sausage laid on your work-board you will see that the lower half curves in at the bottom throughout its length. This is the UNDERCUT. If you covered the whole sausage with plaster, it would run into the undercut and when dry it would, as with the encasement above, be impossible to remove the sausage without breaking the plaster.

The only way to replicate the sausage (i.e. your original) would again involve a waste mould as described above, with all the disadvantages of that process.

If, on the other hand, we cut the sausage in half length-ways and laid the flat surface of one half of the cut sausage on a board, there would be no undercut. When covered with plaster, that mould could be easily lifted once it was dry, and the half sausage removed. *This would be a ONE PIECE MOULD and could be used over and over again* – even were the sausage to be eaten.

Some readers may have spotted that with the halved sausage you could make another similar mould and place the two together to cast a whole sausage. You would need to contrive a small hole at one end through which to pour your casting plaster but *this would be a TWO PIECE MOULD and could, likewise, be used over and over.*

With a clay figure there are several ways of dealing with undercuts:

1. You can fill them in with more clay and, thus, avoid the problem when casting. (It may be possible, later, to restore some indentation to the cast by removing excess material.)

2. You can ignore moderate undercuts and risk casting them in one piece moulds. However, when you lift the mould some of the original will break away. This is not a serious problem (unless you specially want to pre-serve your original itself) because the clay which has come away from the original can be washed out of the mould. Sometimes you can 'get away' with this. The problem usually comes when you fill this mould with plaster for the cast. You will subsequently have two rigid pieces of plaster locked together which cannot be separated without breaking away the outer mould to release the cast; you will be faced, in effect, with a waste mould (see above) but without having used the proper techniques for producing one. The risk is of damaging your cast. (Proper use of a waste mould, I return to shortly on page 62.)

3. You may get around deeper undercuts by making a TWO PIECE MOULD divided appropriately.

4. You might, in such ways as will be described in Chapter 5, alter your original model so as to 'design' out any undercuts.

5. You may simply have to accept the disadvantages and head for a waste mould.

Undercuts can, unfortunately, occur in all types of moulds, including two piece moulds as in 3 above. So look out for their probability, and take care to avoid them or deal with them.

Release Agents

Release agents, to remind you, are introduced to cover the inner surface of a mould so that the subsequent casting can be easily removed. There are several substances which can be used for this purpose and commercial preparations can be purchased, usually in spray cans. Cooking oil, *soft* wax sold as a release agent (wax shoe or furniture polish, of a light or neutral colour and the right consistency, may make a satisfactory substitute), and Vaseline are all sometimes used. Whilst ensuring the inside of the mould is well covered, each of these should be used sparingly, especially Vaseline, as an excess may leave marks on the surface of the cast. If necessary, wipe off any surplus with a paper towel.

I usually employ the following procedure. With an inexpensive small, round, long-handled, long-bristled (no. 14) paintbrush, I prepare the inside of the mould by giving it a good scrubbing with a liquid detergent – I may add a little water to help it flow but this is not essential. Work up a good lather, making sure that the whole surface and all indentations are scrubbed and covered. **DO NOT WIPE OFF THIS LATHER.** Soon you will find it has disappeared – having been absorbed by the plaster. After that, to complete the process, I rub over a thin film of cooking oil or soft wax, or spray the surface quite lightly with a commercial release agent. After a little experience you get a feel for the best way to treat individual moulds before casting.

MAKING MOULDS AND CASTING

Remember, when you begin making any mould, that your clay figure should still be moist. The shape and form of the original figure determines the type of mould.

As revealed in the **Undercuts** section above, a choice needs to be made between a ONE PIECE MOULD, a WASTE MOULD and a TWO PIECE MOULD.

One or two piece moulds can be re-used to make more than one cast. A waste mould can be used only *once* to make a *single* cast, and *the original is destroyed*.

Even with one and two piece moulds, your clay original will not always survive wholly intact, no matter how much care you take. Some originals part from their moulds easily, others not so easily. With the latter you have to abandon keeping the clay original. Instead, you must scoop it out from the mould. (Hence the necessity for the original still being moist.) Use your fingers and a wooden tool. Final, hard-to-get-at remnants of clay should be easy to flush away with water and a brush.

Do not be too concerned about this unavoidable destruction of your original. Once you have a one or two piece mould, you can make as many copies as you wish. Losing the original is simply a common feature of this kind of work.

One Piece Moulds – for relief work, and some reclining figures

This type of work is developed in Chapters 5-8. These subjects suit a one piece mould, being on a flat base and horizontal.

The simplest way to make a one piece mould is to pour Mix 2 plaster (see page 47) over the figure. The lower drawing in Fig. 11 shows this.

It follows that sometimes you may need to prevent your

moulding plaster from spreading out too much – although this is not always necessary, especially with thick plaster.

When you do need to prevent plaster from spreading, you can either: build a low retaining wall of clay around the original; place the original in a suitable container, preferably a plastic box; make a rigid wall specially for it; or use Lego. I will deal with each of these several methods *first*, before coming to the next stages – removal of the original from the mould, and then casting.

Building a Low Retaining Wall

Begin by rolling out a strip of clay about half an inch (just over 1cm) thick and 1 inch (2.5cm) wide. Press this strip firmly on edge around the figure about 1 inch (2.5cm) outside it. The wall does not have to fit the shape of your figure too exactly or be as high.

Once everything is ready, gently dribble Mix 2 moulding plaster over your figure, directing it with your hands. Make sure that you cover the figure completely, you check that the plaster has run into any 'nooks and crannies', and that there are no air pockets.

A useful tip to reach well into deeper crevices is to blow gently on the plaster to encourage it to run in. *Do not attempt to push plaster into these places or you may distort your original.* (You may find it better for achieving good coverage if you use Mix 1 to start with and, when this has dried a little – not absolutely dry – you pour Mix 2 over that first layer. However, this is not usually necessary; it depends upon the figure and whether there are any tricky areas which may trap air.)

Once under way, carry on building up your mould into an oval-shaped mound over the figure until you have good, even cover about three-quarters of an inch (2cm) thick. The exterior need not be smooth. Before it sets entirely, make a small flat surface on the top for it to stand on when casting by drawing a plastic ruler or straight edge along the surface. (See Fig. 11.)

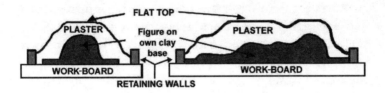

WITHOUT RETAINING WALLS

Fig. 11. One piece moulds.

You must leave your mould to dry completely before attempting to remove the clay original. (I prefer to leave mine overnight.)

Using a Plastic Container

Plastic containers, such as those used for storing food are excellent. Some that I have are quite deep which is useful. They all have the advantage that you can 'flex' the sides to release the mould. The types used for storing bacon are long and rectangular, and a small maquette, like those described in Chapter 6, will fit in them nicely. Look out for other handy sizes to have ready.

Choose a plastic box at least half an inch (1.25cm) higher all round than the figure. Rub the whole inside of this over with a suggestion of cooking oil.

Your model now has to be removed very cautiously, using the piano wire or clay cutter, from the work-board and placed firmly and squarely on the bottom of the box.

Now pour plaster (Mix 2) slowly – to avoid introducing air – over the figure from the bottom upwards up to at least half an inch (1.25cm) thick above the top of your figure, preferably a little more. There is no need to level this top as it will be 'self-levelling'. You may find a little water rises to the top. This can be left or 'blotted' off with a paper towel.

Let the moulding plaster set well (overnight is best) before removing your mould, with its figure still inside, from the plastic container. Then, just tip the container upside down, and gently ease it apart from the contents.

Using a Rigid Wall

There may be times when a low, clay, retaining wall or a plastic box will not meet the task. Instead you must make a rigid wall. The best materials are white-faced chipboard, or MDF (medium-density fibreboard) either of which can be bought from any DIY store.

Cut four sides at least an inch (2.5cm) longer/wider, and three-quarters of an inch (2cm) higher than your figure. (Allow on one pair for the thickness of the material of the other pair.) Join these together with strong adhesive tape, pin nails or screws, so that you have a nice, bottomless, 'box' with square corners. Fix this firmly to your clean work-board either with double-sided tape or by pressing soft wads of clay around the outside edges.

If you have used MDF for your rigid wall, cover this on its inside surfaces with Vaseline or furniture wax. MDF is absorbent so other release agents (see page 52) are not appropriate. If your wall is made with white-faced chipboard Vaseline isn't necessary. Instead, simply use a very sparing touch of cooking oil.

When all is ready you can pour in moulding plaster. Use Mix 2, as with the plastic container, but consider starting with Mix 1 if you have any concerns about good coverage. Your plaster needs to reach into every inlet without trapping air, and to rise a full half inch (1.25cm) above the top of your figure.

Once more, it is best to leave the mould overnight so as to be certain the plaster is fully dry, before dismantling this wall – or trying to remove your original.

Using a Lego Wall

For this alternative, fix a bottom course of Lego bricks to your work-board with double-sided adhesive tape, or place some wads of soft clay around it to prevent it from moving.

Next build your Lego wall up to the desirable height – so that the moulding plaster can fill up to be a full half inch (1.25cm) above your figure.

Pour in the moulding plaster, following the guidelines I have already given. There is no need to oil the inside surfaces of a Lego wall because, once the mould is properly dry, Lego easily separates from it. 'Demolishing' the wall next day is therefore simple.

Removing the Clay Original from the Mould

This is not difficult although you must proceed cautiously or you may damage the mould.

If you used a low, clay retaining wall around your mould, that wall should 'peel' away quite easily. The mould and its contents should then come free from the work-board surface easily but, if the whole thing is stuck on by suction, you may need to dislodge it with your piano wire cutter (held taut) or, very gently, using a blunt knife. *Don't up-end the mould yet.*

You won't have the above problem at all if you used a plastic container (from which the mould and its contents are easily parted as explained already).

If you used a rigid or a Lego wall, you will need to dismantle it first and then make sure the mould and figure are safely separated from the work-board itself. (Do this as suggested above.)

Next you can lift your mould, *with its contents inside*, a little way off your work-board – or, for a mould previously removed from a plastic container, turn it gently upside down. This is the moment when, if you are both lucky and careful, your original figure may drop cleanly – undamaged – from your mould with a little tap or a shake but without much further ado. If so, good. You can keep or discard it as you wish. If not – as probably happens more often – you will have to abandon your clay original.

Invert the mould, so that it can stand upside down on the flat top you made. Next scoop out as much clay as you can with your fingers. A wooden tool may help to get at any small corners or crevices. You need not be too fussy as the next stage will complete the job. This is to wash out all the remaining clay with a soft brush and plenty of water. You may find a little discoloration inside the mould, as many of the clays contain dye; but don't worry. You should now have a very nice, clean mould even if it is discoloured internally.

Casting in the One Piece Mould

We must now consider how to cast, or make, the final figure. This appears to be quite simple. All you need to do is to pour some plaster into the mould you have just made – sounds easy. However, there are some pitfalls which could ruin your efforts and *which you must take into account*. So, follow these instructions carefully:

1.   First, you must ensure that the mould is quite clean;
      free from any residual clay or debris which may have
      dropped in. Then you must prepare it. After you have
      removed all the clay (as fully described above) give the
      mould A GOOD SCRUBBING INSIDE WITH LIQ-
      UID DETERGENT. You can add a little water if you
      feel like it but this is not always necessary. I do this job
      with a small, round, long-handled, long-bristled (no.
      14) painting brush. Scrub until you see a distinct
      lather arising – making sure you go into all the cor-
      ners. **DO NOT REMOVE THIS LATHER.** Leave it to
      dry out and soon it will disappear. This process not
      only further cleans the mould thoroughly but will also
      help to release the cast later on.

2.   Now you must apply a release agent to the whole
      inside surface. My section on page 52 reviews different
      types. Which one you use depends upon your choice
      and the particular subject mould. If you are in any
      doubt, I recommend the soft white wax for most
      projects in this book. Rub the wax well in, with the
      finger, or a smooth, lint free cloth. Make sure no
      surplus is left showing or it will be seen on the cast.
      Also make sure it goes into every nook and cranny. You
      can achieve this with a small paintbrush but make sure
      no excess is left behind – otherwise this will leave a gap,
      or hole, in the cast.

3.   Make up your plaster for casting in the same way used
      for moulding plaster described earlier in this chapter.
      You may use a little Mix 1 and, mainly, Mix 2.

You are now nearly ready to pour in the casting plaster but,
first, I must give a little further cautionary advice. When you
mix your plaster, do it as gently as possible to avoid introducing air. You want to avoid air bubbles infiltrating the

mix and/or pockets of air becoming trapped within the mould.

I never lift my wooden mixing spoon above the surface. Remember there will be some air, anyway, as not only does water contain air but some air will be introduced as you pour in the plaster. I'm afraid this is a nuisance but with plaster I know of no sure way of removing it all. You will see some air bubbles rise to the surface after mixing your plaster but you cannot leave it too long, waiting for them all to rise, or it will set. A little shaking or banging the mixing bowl on the table will help the bubbles to rise.

When you pour plaster into your mould, air also gets trapped into corners or in the ends of projections seen on the original model. Those parts, like fingers, legs and noses, which form the deepest recesses within the mould, are the most vulnerable. As plaster runs into any of these recesses, any air which cannot escape will create a nasty void without plaster at the extremity. This will result, for example, in a missing end of a toe or finger on your final cast. The best way to overcome this is:

4.   Pour in a little very thin (Mix 1) plaster first. Roll this around the mould to reach well into all these crevices before adding the final, Mix 2, plaster. Again, don't leave it too long before doing so. YOUR FIRST LAYER MUST NOT DRY OUT. Indeed, it will be absorbed by, and wants to become part of, the final casting plaster. Its only purpose is to 'reach those parts which other plaster will not reach'.

Before pouring in Mix 2 make sure your mould is standing firm on a flat surface and is quite level. (Sometimes, I even use a spirit level for this.) If necessary prop it up with some wads of clay. The last thing you want is for it to fall over as you are pouring in your casting plaster.

5.   Pour Mix 2 *slowly and carefully* into your mould. I nearly always transfer my plaster to a jug with a spout for this purpose, so that I can control the flow and direction. Try to fill from the bottom of the mould upwards so as to 'push' out the air and not trap it. It is best to overfill the mould, a little, and then level off the top by drawing a ruler across it.

Whilst you do not have a lot of time for this whole operation, I never rush it. Act slowly and deliberately, preparing as much as you can in advance, clearing the work space of any likely encumbrance and thinking out the sequence of operations. (Here is a novel tip: when the cast is almost dry you can 'polish' or smooth the exposed surface with a slightly damp trowel. I have a tiny one – such as you can buy in DIY shops – which is ideal for doing this. A smooth base on which to stand it will be helpful should you later wish to mount your cast figure.)

It is very difficult to say how long it will take a plaster cast to set, there are so many variables – size, temperature, humidity, precise water/plaster ratio, even the age of the plaster powder. You just have to be patient and wait until you feel sure it is quite dry all through. I really prefer to leave mine 24 hours but I appreciate how anxious you may be to see your final result.

Removing the Final Cast from the Mould

If you have followed the instructions above you should not have any difficulty. You may find that, once you invert the mould, it will simply fall out – be careful it does not drop too far – but a *gentle* tapping might help. If it does stick, try a little more tapping all round. If that doesn't work, pour a little hot water over the outside of the mould. This will expand the mould a little, which should allow the cast to come free.

When your final, cast figure does emerge, especially if it is your first one ever, you will feel quite proud and emotional. (I don't want to tell too many personal stories but, on one occasion when I exhibited a work, a lady came up to me and said, 'It looks as if you were in love with it.' I said, 'I was.')

Should you find some air holes on the surface of your final figure, they can usually be filled easily, using thick, Mix 3 plaster. Dampen the area a little first. An alternative might be to use Polyfilla. However, I'm afraid neither attempt at repair will generally work very well, if at all, at the ends of extremities.

The above general principles apply to all casting but they are dealt with again, in respect of particular problems, when we come to the appropriate subject.

Waste Moulds – use for simple reliefs or when undercuts may be a problem

Waste moulds are very similar to one piece moulds but have two disadvantages in that only one cast can ever be made (because the mould has to be broken away from the finished cast and is, thus, destroyed – or 'wasted'), and, secondly, that you lose your original figure. The great advantage to set against these is that you can, with care, cast undercuts, detail and indentations.

The next difference occurs when applying the plaster. With a waste mould it is usual to apply the plaster in TWO LAYERS, the first one being quite thin and slightly tinted. This enables you to spot where the original is when breaking the mould away from the final cast.

Procedure

Before mixing your moulding plaster for the first, thin layer, add a little colour to the water. YELLOW OCHRE POWDER COLOUR is usually used for this. If you are unable to get this from an art shop or DIY merchant, use a little acrylic colour. The tinting weakens the strength of the plaster slightly so use a very small amount of colour. You should hardly be able to see the difference in the colour of your water. Make up some Mix 1 plaster using the coloured water. Run this tinted plaster THINLY over your figure, ensuring that all parts, undercuts and crevices, are covered. If necessary, use my tip given earlier, and blow this tinted layer of plaster gently into the corners, inlets and undercuts to ensure that it runs in everywhere. *Do not spread the plaster with a brush as this may damage the original.* Remember, this layer is going to be the essential mould of your figure and that it will be very thin and brittle when dry. The next layer is mainly to support and strengthen it.

It is not absolutely essential to use a retaining wall or box at any stage in making a waste mould. Just allow the plaster to run off and spread out a little. However, you must work carefully or you will have plaster 'all over the place'!

When the first layer is quite dry, apply a plain white, second layer, using Mix 2. This must be applied carefully, because the *first* layer, which should be not much thicker than an egg shell, may easily break. Once again, ensure that the whole figure is completely covered. The thickness of the outer layer should depend upon the size of the original but it does not have to be too thick for small figures. About three-quarters of an inch (2cm) thick is sufficient. As with a one piece mould, make a flat surface on the top of this outer layer and then leave your completed waste mould until its plaster is absolutely dry.

Removal of your Clay Figure from its Waste Mould

First, invert the waste mould and stand it on the flat surface you made. Handle it at all times with great care as the inner, coloured layer is so thin and vulnerable. Now, remove as much of the clay original as you can, with your fingers. (As I explained earlier, you always have to sacrifice your original from a waste mould.) Continue carefully, again so as not to damage that first thin layer of plaster, using a wooden tool. Finally, wash out any remainder with a soft brush and plenty of water, using a little detergent if necessary, making sure you go into every nook and cranny and that the mould is eventually absolutely clean. Before you can make your cast you *must* allow the entire plaster of your mould to dry out completely.

Casting in the Waste Mould

When you are sure it is quite dry inside, you need to prepare it for the cast – as with other types of mould. First wash the whole inside carefully with detergent, and when the lather has been absorbed, apply a little release agent (see page XX).

Pour in your plaster for the cast by running (as described from page XX) a thin Mix 1 round the whole of the inside of your mould as the first step, before filling up – carefully, to avoid any air pockets from becoming trapped – with Mix 2.

Revealing the Final Cast

When quite cold and set, invert your waste mould again and, with the bottom of your cast now on your work-board, start to break away the top (thicker) layer of the plaster mould. Do this with a small hammer and a wood chisel which is not too sharp. Apply the chisel at near right angles to the plaster mould and tap gently. After a little tapping a small piece of the top layer should break off. Continue to break off small pieces at a time. Sometimes it may have a little of the coloured second layer attached. Don't worry about this – but you must be very careful not to damage your figure. Finally, you should reach a stage where all that remains to be removed is the coloured layer. This resembles the shell of a hard-boiled egg and should be easily removable with a fingernail or a small knife. A little cleaning up all round thereafter should leave you with a very fine cast of your original work.

Two Piece Moulds – for more difficult pieces and figures 'in the round'

Two piece moulds are necessary when a single mould cannot be removed in one piece because there are serious undercuts, cavities or holes in the work, or because you want to cast the whole figure 'in the round' – that is in three dimensions including all sides.

There are some limitations as, for example, with the whole sausage on page 50. More difficult still would be if you wanted to make a mould of, say, an apple – because of the indentation for the stalk. If you 'halved' your apple 'vertically' along the line of its core and placed the two halves cut-surface down for moulding, this indentation would still prevent you from lifting either of the part moulds away from the final cast. You could make the mould in two 'horizontal' halves; one for the top of the apple where the stalk enters and one for the bottom. Then each part mould would lift easily enough. However, if your objective was to bring the two parts together to cast one complete apple, you would have to leave a hole through which to pour the casting plaster.

I hasten to add, however, that snags such as these are quite rare. You won't normally find problems you cannot resolve. It is conventional to call the two pieces when joined together 'The Mould' and to refer to each piece as a section or part.

There are two distinct ways of making a two piece mould:

HORIZONTALLY or VERTICALLY. Which to choose depends upon the size and shape of your work. Small figures can be made horizontally – which is the easiest way – but larger figures and heads may have to be moulded vertically, which is more difficult.

Separation

In either event, before the original figure dries out and before you start, you must decide where the separation between the two parts is best going to be. Where you separate them is critical because the join between them may remain visible on the cast. Often this can be removed at the finishing stage but it is not always possible to eradicate it entirely. Therefore it is important to choose where it will least show on the cast or, if its removal later is likely to be difficult, where it will least matter. You must also consider how each part can be removed easily without any problematic undercuts preventing you from doing so.

Usually, this separation will follow the line of the highest points of the model, dividing it roughly in half but do not stick to this principle too rigidly; find the line which is most suitable.

Score your separation line with the end of a pointed modelling tool, skewer or some such handy tool. Take care as you do this. I seldom do it in one sweep, preferring to make several small lines along critical points, which I can then join together. An example is in Fig. 33 on page 134. One of the advantages of clay is that, if you do make a mistake or want to make a change, then you can easily smooth over the damp clay and replace the line. The line needs to extend round the entire figure *except for the flat bottom on which it stands*. This bit – even if quite small – has to remain open for pouring in your casting plaster.

To sum up: your task comprises making two sections which will fit tightly together in such a way that, when joined as one, two piece mould, they will be easy to fill with plaster and, later, when the cast has set, easy to separate.

Horizontal Method – mostly used for small standing figures with a flat bottom

Whilst there are several ways of making horizontal two piece moulds, for the beginner the easiest method is by laying the figure in a horizontal position on a bed of clay. You then build a platform of clay around the figure. There's a bit more to it but, before that, there are some preparations to be made.

Start, after making your separation line, by carefully covering the back half of your figure with *cling film* – the half you are NOT going to cover first with plaster. Do not tighten the cling film too hard or press it into any recesses or dimples. A simple, overall layer is all that is required. It may help if you next wipe your whole work-board surface over with a thin film of cooking oil (to prevent clay sticking on it). Then make a rough bed of pliable clay on your board and gently lay the figure, cling film-side down, on top of it. The depth of the bed of clay below your figure depends upon its size but it should be not less than half an inch (1.25cm) – allow more for larger figures.

Now, build up a platform of clay around/on top of this rough bed, about 1 inch (2.5cm) wide to line up along the whole length of the separation line on your original figure. The inside edge of this platform must be in contact with the cling film where it abuts the figure and fit snugly.

Keep building up the platform until you reach the separation line, following any contours in that line as necessary. Snip off surplus cling film above the line with a pair of nail scissors or using a Stanley knife but being careful not to damage your figure, and tuck any you can't remove back down just below the surface of your platform.

The next task is to make the top surface of your clay platform smooth by running a kitchen knife, lightly oiled with cooking oil, over it. Now make some 'keys' in this surface to ensure that the second half of the two piece mould will fit tightly and match up to the first half. Form them by pressing some small, half-spherical holes into the surface whilst the clay remains pliable. For this purpose, you can use the tip of your small finger, or you may prefer the round end of a pencil, screwdriver handle or other tool which you may have to hand. (I once used a glass marble stuck to the end of a golf tee!) Position the holes about an inch and a half (3.75cm) apart and half an inch (1.25cm) away from the figure. Do not make them too deep – just less than a half sphere will do. Rub a little cooking oil on your finger or whatever tool you use, and rotate it a little to make a nice, smooth, round recess or 'cup' for each one.

With your platform ready you now need to build a retaining wall closely round the outside of the platform and also *abutting the flat bottom of the figure directly*. This wall, which will hold the plaster when you pour it in, needs to rise at least half an inch (1.5cm) above the highest point of your figure. There are several ways of doing this:

1.   By making a 'box'. The best material for this is white-faced chipboard because, if you cover the insides with a thin film of cooking oil, neither plaster nor clay should then stick to it. The sides can be 'butted' together and joined with pin nails, strong adhesive tape or screws. There is no need to make a bottom for your 'box' as it will rest directly on your work-board but do make sure any gaps between the two are filled in with clay to prevent plaster running out.

You also need to backfill, roughly, with clay, any space that is left between the platform and your wall, up as far as the height of the platform. The side of your wall where it touches the flat bottom of your figure directly *must make uniformly good contact*. If necessary, by using Vaseline (or a smidgen of clay) make a special seal between the two to prevent plaster entering. It is through this corresponding area on each part of your two piece mould that your final casting plaster will be poured.

2.   You can build a 'box' from Lego, as I have in Fig. 12. The advantage of this is that you need first build it only as high as your clay platform. This enables you to backfill and put finishing touches to your platform more easily. You can then build your wall on up, reaching as high as you need your first plaster mould to be. As with a chipboard wall, you may need to seal between the flat clay bottom of your original and the Lego wall touching that – to stop plaster running in between.

3.   If your figure is not too high, you can use slabs of clay standing on end for your walls. Clay being so malleable this method may prove the quickest, with less backfilling needed. (You need not worry, either, with this method, that your slab wall where it fits against the flat bottom of your figure will become stuck to that – or that plaster may seep between the two – as long as there is good contact. In practice, the two need only be pressed together firmly enough to prevent seepage from above. When it comes to its removal, later on, the slab peels away quite satisfactorily.)

Pouring the First Part

When you are sure that your retaining walls are sound and secure, that they, your platform and your figure, are snug with each other in every respect, that your keys are inserted and that the whole structure is level, pour in moulding plaster (Mix 2). Fill up carefully inside the retaining wall, to a good half an inch (1.25cm) thick above the figure. Keep an eye, as you fill, that plaster does run into any recesses uniformly, so that no air gets trapped.

When this has quite set you will be ready to make the second part mould which, naturally, must fit exactly with the first part.

DO NOT REMOVE THE ORIGINAL FROM THE PART MOULD YOU HAVE JUST MADE. Turn the whole thing upside down and stand it on a flat surface. (You may first have to use your clay cutter or piano wire to break the adhesion between the original rough bed of clay and your work-board.)

Your figure is now lying the other way up, hidden under the rough bed of clay and supported by the mould you have just made. You should be able to remove the rough bed of clay, together with the clay platform, if not in one piece, at least without much trouble and without damage to your figure. Remove the cling film too. Peel it away carefully. (Sometimes – though not often – you can do all this without having to dismantle any part of the retaining wall.)

Check the 'keys' you made are now protruding from the plaster with no residual clay adhering. Make sure this half of your figure is clean and free from debris. Apply a little release agent onto the surface of the first mould plaster where the joint will be, including over the keys. Then restore any retaining wall taken down.

Pouring the Second Part

When you are quite sure that all is secure and level and that no plaster will escape, pour Mix 2 plaster over this half of

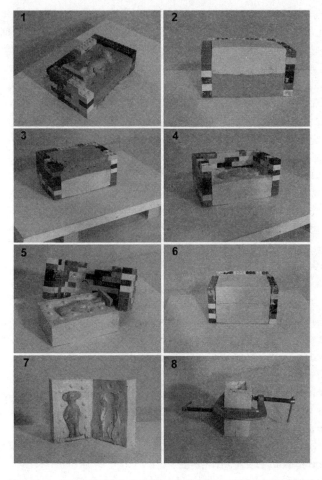

Fig. 12. Horizontal two piece mould with Lego retaining box (front wall removed).

1. Original, lying on a bed of clay. Note key marks.
2. Plaster applied.
3. Inverted.
4. Clay base removed leaving figure in place.
5. Lego retaining box removed for demonstration.
6. Second layer of plaster applied.
7. Two piece mould parted for removal of original.
8. Clamped for cast plaster to be poured through opening at top.

your figure, ensuring as before that the whole of it is completely covered to a minimum half inch (1.25cm) depth and that no air pockets occur. Wait for this second part mould to become really dry; then you can remove the entire retaining wall.

Your two piece mould is now complete and you should have no difficulty in separating the two sections. If there is a problem, soak the whole thing in water for a while – preferably warm water – and use a blunt kitchen knife to prise them apart and reveal the original.

As previously explained, you may not retrieve your original figure wholly intact – but that's what your mould is *for* – to cast a replica, or several if you wish. Nonetheless, if you want to keep the original and you are very careful, you may be lucky.

Casting in the Horizontal Two Piece Mould

Clean out the inside of each part mould, prepare it and treat it with release agent, as explained under that section, on page 52.

Now join the two parts together. When you offer one to the other make quite sure that you have treated both joint faces with release agent, that there is no clay or grit interfering with the join and that the male and female keys are aligned and firmly in place.

The two parts must be held tightly together. There are several ways of doing this:

1. You can buy suitable clamp irons for this job from a specialist supplier.

2. Use 'G' clamps if you have them. This is quite a good method but make sure the clamps do not slip off as you tighten them; and *do not screw them up too tightly* or

you may break your mould.

3.   You can use strong string to make a tourniquet.

4.   You can use strips of car inner tube like elastic bands.
      (Cut across the inner tube at right angles to make each
      strip. You can make dozens of these from one tube.)
      This is quite an effective method for small moulds but
      do make sure the moulds are very tight together.

5.   Strong adhesive, 'duck' tape, can be used but be careful
      that you pull the two halves securely and firmly
      together as you apply the tape.

When you are happy that the mould is rigid and leak-proof,
prop it up safely on end. Make certain that the opening at
the base, now uppermost, is level because this will ensure
that your finished cast will stand up properly. Follow the
same instructions for the casting process which I gave from
item 3 on page 59, under *Casting in the One Piece Mould*.

   Be sure to wait for your cast fully to set before opening up
the mould to reveal your reward. That final stage I will come
to in a moment (page 79) but first I want to introduce you
to vertical, two piece moulds.

*Vertical Method – mostly for larger, free-standing figures and
full-size heads*

When it is not convenient to cast your figure horizontally,
you must do it vertically. One reason might be that you
don't want to risk lifting your figure off the work-board
because of its size and weight.

   Whatever the reason, you are unable with this method to
make a surrounding platform or a retaining wall; neither
will you initially be able to pour your moulding plaster
because there will be nothing there to contain it. Instead,

you have to flick the plaster on gently with your fingers.

This can be a bit messy. Cover the floor – and everything else in sight – with old newspapers, which are easy to clear up later. Another idea is to work within a 'casting cabinet' – a television or washing machine packing box will suit this purpose. Cut the front and the top off, place your model within and all the surplus plaster which gets thrown around will be contained.

Again, the first thing to do – as explained on page 66 – is to mark your separation line. This is a little tricky with a head. I have seen moulds made where the line runs straight down the centre of the face. There may, sometimes, be good reasons for this but it will tend to leave a nasty division mark which will be difficult to remove, especially in places like the lips and nose. So, it is best to make the division across the head, behind the ears, and running down the neck, where it is less likely to show and can more easily be erased. The division does not have to be straight but can follow the contours of the subject where this is simpler.

With the separation line marked you now have to make a partition, which will divide your two, part sections. This can be done in one of two ways:

1. With shims.

2. With clay.

1. *Shims.* (This method can only be used on a clay – or Plasticine – figure whilst the material remains soft.) Shims are very thin strips, usually of metal, used to separate the two halves. See Fig. 13. Most professionals and those who do a lot of work use shims made of a thin, non-ferrous metal, like brass, which can be used time and time again. If you can find some thin metal sheet of this kind, cut it into strips about 1¼ inches (3cm) wide and then into rectangular pieces about 2

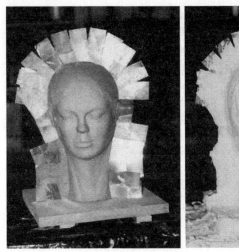

Fig. 13. Use of shims.
Left: Metal shims inserted in clay.
Right: Head covered in plaster.

inches (5cm) long. You can also make shims from old film negatives. Again, cut them into roughly 2-inch (5cm) lengths by 1¼ inches (3cm) wide.

Insert the strips firmly into your clay figure so that they follow the separation line, and stand out from the figure at right angles, making sure that they overlap well – about half an inch (1.25cm) will be fine. With shims, there is no need to make keys for the two halves to lock together. The shims leave a ridged surface which itself will serve this purpose.

2. *Clay.* Make strips of clay by rolling out a slab about three-quarters of an inch (2cm) thick and then cutting this lengthways – each strip being cut about 1 inch (2.5cm) wide. Press the strip on to your model fairly firmly but not enough to distort the figure. You need

to position the strip, thin edge to your figure, carefully, so that one of the rolled-flat faces runs along your separation line. Make sure any joins in the strips are held firmly together.

Unlike with shims, you must now make keys to ensure that the two parts of the mould will lock together. On the surface of your clay partition adjacent to the separation line that is FACING the direction you are going to apply plaster for the first mould – make the necessary small, half-spherical indentations (see page 68).

Making the First Part Mould

Now, flick Mix 1 plaster onto that half of the figure with your fingers, making sure the keyed face of the clay partition is also covered – but not its outside edge. If you have used shims, it doesn't matter on which side of your figure you start because there are no keys to worry about.

This is quite a tricky operation but not difficult. This first coat of thin plaster must go into every corner and crevice – and the key holes if present. If necessary, make sure of this as before, by blowing on the plaster before it sets. As with any mould, you cannot brush or push it on, because that would risk leaving marks on your original which would be seen on your final cast.

You have to work fairly quickly with this first coat. Keep the blank side of your partition, as well as the external edge, clean. Wipe any surplus plaster off as you proceed.

When this first coat has set, apply more layers of plaster, now using Mix 2. Aim to cover the half figure with plaster about 1 inch (2.5cm) thick. Build the plaster up a little thicker close to the partition – for extra strength should a little force be required later, when separating the two halves. A Mix 3 consistency suits well for this last purpose, as you can press it lightly in place by hand.

Making the Second Part Mould

When the above first covering of plaster is entirely dry you have to make the second part mould.

First, remove the partition BUT LEAVE THE MOULD YOU HAVE MADE IN PLACE.

If you are using shims these now have to be lifted out vertically with some care. (I use long-nose pliers for this.)

A clay partition should strip away quite easily, leaving your keys standing proud on the face of the first part mould where the second part will butt against it for the casting stage. Clean off, thoroughly, all traces of clay still adhering to that face or having stuck to the figure itself – taking care all the time not to damage your figure.

You should next apply release agent to that joint face of the first mould. A thin film of cooking oil or commercial spray will do fine. However, some sculptors use a dilute solution of clay and water, which you could also try for this purpose.

Now apply plaster to the second half of the figure as you did the first.

When the second part mould is dry and cold – the longer you leave it the better – the two sections can be separated. They should come apart fairly easily but, as before, you may have to ease them a little with a blunt tool. If you have further difficulty, you may first need to remove the whole thing from your work-board, then put the entire mould in a plastic bucket and give it a good soaking in warm water.

Unlike one piece or horizontal two piece moulds, where you remove the clay from the mould, here you remove the

mould from the clay – by easing it off. Often, in my experience, this will leave the original in good condition and,
depending on the clay used and other circumstances – like
heat and humidity – it will keep indefinitely. (Figs. 43 left
and 46 are the originals from which casts were made, and
they are still, after many years, in good condition.)

Casting in the Vertical Two Piece Mould

Having separated the two part mould(s) you must, as usual,
thoroughly remove any remaining clay. Clean up the inte-
rior of the moulds with a household paintbrush and plenty
of water. Make sure no clay remains hidden anywhere
within the moulds. When clean, prepare the insides and the
two joint faces, as with previous types, by scrubbing with
detergent, until it lathers. Let that dry and then apply a
release agent. (See page 52.)

Now join the two halves exactly as directed for horizontal
two piece moulds (on page 72) ensuring that they are tightly
locked together and that no plaster can seep out between
them at the join. This good fit is more critical than with the
horizontal two piece mould. With a horizontal two piece
mould that has leaked, a little remedial action may be
possible on the cast but this is much more difficult when
the two piece mould is vertical.

When you are quite sure it is safe to proceed, carefully
prop up the inverted, firmly locked, mould. (I usually jam
a full-sized head in a plastic bucket.) As with the horizontal two piece mould and for the same reason, make
sure the opening at the base, now uppermost, is level.
(Page 73 refers.) Pour in your casting plaster through this
opening. Use the same casting mix of plaster and the same
general techniques deployed casting in any mould (see
from page 58 if necessary) but you may need to take extra
care with what you do with larger figures on account of

their weight. For example, as always, try to reach the bottom of the mould first to avoid trapped air. If your mould is quite big it is preferable not to pour all the plaster at one time. Pour about a third and then, if possible, grasp the mould and swirl it around – tilting it as you do so – to ensure the plaster reaches every corner, nook and cranny. (With a full-size head this becomes quite heavy and difficult to do, so I usually seek assistance.) Then carefully continue the pouring until the mould is full.

Make sure the cast is *cold* before attempting to remove it from its mould. Preferably leave it 24 hours.

Opening up a Two Piece Mould to Reveal the Final Cast

This must be done with great care. An assistant may prove invaluable because the whole assembly may, now, be quite heavy and, of course, you must make sure you do not drop it. With a large piece I grasp one side whilst a colleague holds the other, and we work together pulling the two pieces apart – trying not to twist it, as this may damage both the mould and the cast. A stuck mould can be stubborn – mine usually are – so be patient.

The first step is to try to pull your mould open horizontally. If you are having problems, it may help if you pour water into the join through a hosepipe. Or (*at your own risk*) use instead a kettle of very hot water. The latter sometimes will expand the plaster of the mould a little faster than that of the cast. If all else fails, then a couple of blunt chisels may help start the process once you can penetrate the join in a couple of places. Tap them in and then twist very, very gently. Once the suction is broken, the moulds usually come apart quite easily.

With a large cast, like a head, you will get a great feeling of elation when your figure finally emerges. Clean up the cast generally, and carefully remove any join marks which may be showing. A blunt chisel, kitchen knife or similar tool may be suitable for this purpose.

If you have damaged the cast a little during the prising apart, you can usually repair this with Mix 3 plaster or a domestic filler, neither of which will probably show if, as suggested in the next section, you colour the finished cast.

Once you are satisfied with the clean up, you can finish off, where necessary, with very fine abrasive paper used very gently. Abrasive papers are sold in various degrees of 'roughness' called 'grit'. For this purpose you need about a 400 grit to start with; then perhaps follow that with 800 grit paper. The number represents the quantity of grinding particles to a given area. The larger the particles, the fewer there are and the smaller the grade number. For example, 1,000 grit is very fine. You can buy abrasive papers in any good DIY shop. You don't have to be too fussy about the amount of grit; if they haven't got what you want, near enough will do.

COLOURING YOUR CAST

Your cast will be a rather dull, white, chalky looking affair and you may want to put some life and colour into it. Adding colour to work, even that cast in metals such as bronze, is usual. Most untouched metal castings are pretty lack-lustre unless some colour or texture is added.

There are several ways of doing this on metal but they all involve a chemical process. Sculpture in metal is beyond our scope here but it is as well to know that this process is called PATINATION. I will, therefore, use this same term when colouring plaster to look like metal – which I prefer – even though, strictly, it is not the correct term.

Other kinds of painting will enable you to transform your

casts perhaps in several colours, like the porcelain figurines seen in souvenir and chinaware shops.

1. Painting

If you decide to paint your figure, it is a good idea to seal it first. This can be done with a little fixative, which can be bought from art shops in spray cans. Use an acrylic or similar paint. Water or oil colours are not suitable. When you have finished painting, spray with two or three more coats of fixative.

Another painted finish which can be very attractive is achieved by an overall covering with emulsion paint. It is not, generally, necessary to seal the surface first if using emulsion paint but, before you paint it on, choose the colour carefully. A light buff or stone colour would be suitable but you may care to experiment with more exotic colours. If you do not like the colour you have chosen you can usually paint over it, but be careful with reds and blues; they are difficult to obliterate.

Interesting mottled textures can be achieved by spraying, or by flicking-on, another colour. Let the emulsion paint dry first. Then you can either use an artists' or model-makers' spray gun, a blow diffuser (both of which can also be bought in art shops), or a toothbrush.

A blow diffuser is quite cheap. It consists of two tubes joined together by a 'swivel joint'. You place the free end of the long tube in the paint and blow through the shorter one. This is great fun and I have used them often for all manner of art work.

Almost any type of paint may be used but it may have to be thinned quite a bit with water, before use in the spray gun or the diffuser. I prefer emulsion paint. You can buy small pots of 'trial' colours and these are ideal for this purpose. Using a toothbrush is also great fun and is an old technique used by many of the Impressionists. Dip the brush in the colour, hold it about 6 inches (15cm) away from your figure and then draw a finger across the bristles so that the colour 'flicks' on to it. With either spray or toothbrush do not make the 'splatters' too small or too close together. With practice, you can vary the size on the same piece. Practise on a piece of paper or card first. (With all the work in this book, experimentation and trial and error are essential. That, for me, is part of the creative process. When you just do as you are told, you are making less use of your own creativity.)

2. 'Patination' – giving your cast plaster figure a 'bronze' effect

There are several ways of doing this and none is difficult.

(a) You can buy special kits, with instructions, from art shops. These usually give a very pleasing effect.

(b) You can buy special bronze-coloured powder which is applied using a brush or cloth dipped in methylated spirit. This is quite good but leaves a rather monotonous surface which, when dry, benefits from further treatment using one of the techniques suggested below.

(c) You can use paints as suggested under **Painting** but restricting the colours to browns and ochres. Special paints can now be bought from art shops for painting on plaster but emulsion paints are quite successful for this and can be applied by brush or spray.

Whichever method you use you will need more than one colour to obtain a good finish. Cover your figure with a base colour like burnt umber. When dry, cover with a lighter, earth colour, like raw sienna, but wipe a good deal of this off with a crumpled rag or paper before it dries. Next you need to darken the cavities – this can be done simply by using one of the dark-coloured proprietary tints. Alternatively, graphite powder or stove polish can be used. Brush a little on, then brush off as much as you can, leaving just a delicate 'patina' in the crevices. Now, brighten the high spots. You can buy a special 'gold' wax, in tubes or sticks, for this purpose. Apply a little to the top surfaces, gently rub this in with your finger or a cloth and wipe off any surplus.

The above suggestions will produce a fairly effective imitation bronze but you do need to experiment a little and mustn't be afraid to use odd materials which you think might be effective. I have often used shoe polish but there are more ideas below. It is usually best to FIX the finished result with a spray fixative.

3. Some More Finishes for Cast Plaster

(a) Mix half a cup of full cream milk – or thin cream – with a pinch of yellow ochre powder and a few grains of burnt sienna. Stir well to dissolve the powder. Rub well in, with a cloth or clean shoe brush and buff up (polish well) when dry.

(b) Burnish all over with brown shoe polish, from a tin, as you would your shoes. Use your 'polishing' brush to 'remove' the soft excess polish. Once 'clean', add highlights with gold wax – as mentioned above. Finish with a spray fixative.

(c) Spray lightly with red, rust inhibitor. When dry, burnish over the top with a mixture of soft white wax (furniture polish will do – or even shoe polish) and graphite powder. Buff up when finished. It is a matter of choice whether or not you spray over a fixative. This is not necessary if, when dry, the colour does not come off on your hands but it does give a more shiny finish which some people prefer.

(d)　Mix a third of a cup of shellac with an equal amount of methylated spirit; stir well to dissolve, and add ¼ teaspoon each of violet and viridian pigments. (If you cannot make up the shellac mixture use button polish – which is itself virtually the same.) Cover your figure with this and, if you feel inclined, darken the cavities and brighten the high spots as described in 2 on page 83. Either way, burnish the result with a little white furniture wax mixed with graphite powder and buff up as in (c) above.

I have emphasised the need to experiment – but you don't want to ruin your work. So, always test new materials on old plaster moulds or some left-over plaster which, rather than throw it away, you may have previously cast in a plastic box for use in carving as described in Chapter 11.

MOUNTING A MODEL

Many figures stand quite well alone without being mounted but, if you feel a mount will enhance your figure, a nice piece of bevelled, polished, hard wood will be fine. Attach your figure to its mount using an epoxy resin.

Marble and other stone mounts are not really a subject for this book but I have given the name of a supplier in the Appendix as you may find them suitable for smaller figures. My Fig. 25, Nascença, is mounted on polished stone.

For smaller work, stick the figure to the mount with an epoxy resin adhesive. If you are using a wooden mount it is best to fix it to your figure *before* treating the mount with varnish or wax polish.

If you wish to prevent your figure from scratching furniture surfaces you can cover the bottom of a mounting block, or that of a free standing figure, with 'flock' paper which has an adhesive backing; sold in DIY shops.

There is more about casting and mounting in subsequent chapters as the subject arises.

Chapter 5:

Relief Work

Our next step is into relief work. For the purpose of this book, relief work is taken to mean sculpture developed from a flat background which, itself, remains an essential part of the work. I am suggesting this now, as opposed to full, three-dimensional figures, because relief work is simpler to execute and cast. Three-dimensional figures 'in the round' may need supporting armatures (internal frameworks) and can be quite a lot more difficult to work on and to cast. Therefore it is a good idea, to begin with, to work on subjects – even the human body – in relief. In this way you can become acquainted with anatomy and proportions without having to get involved in armature building.

Relief work can be executed either in malleable materials, such as clay, or in solid substances, like marble. *In this chapter we are only going to work with clay*. In Chapter 11 we will consider carving 'reliefs' in a solid material: cast plaster.

Relief work is conceivably the oldest form of carving – probably dating back to the time when man first scratched out images on the walls of his cave dwellings – and it has been used by sculptors, including the greatest, ever since.

Relief sculpture is generally divided into the following styles:

Intaglio which is cut below the background surface and used these days mainly for lettering.

Base or **Low Relief** where the modelling, whilst all above that surface remains quite shallow.

High Relief where the modelling is more fully developed. There are also intermediary levels, described as **Mezzo Relief**.

Some sculptors have used more than one style; combining, for example, low relief for the background and high relief for figures in the foreground (see Fig. 16). The style and depth of working will depend upon the individual and the subject. It is as well to know these terms but don't let them influence your work at this stage. Low relief is probably the most difficult – being not far removed from drawing 'in three dimensions' but with the added difficulty of trying to execute depth on a shallow surface. The first exercises which I suggest will be more in the intermediary level, **Mezzo Relief**. However, you need not decide on one style to the exclusion of another. Just work naturally; let your work flow and see what results.

The main objectives of this chapter are to:

Increase your familiarity with clay.

Introduce working from a flat surface.

Consider shape and form, in a third dimension.

Practise one piece casting in plaster.

The choice of subjects must be your own. We all have different preferences. Your style and interests will develop gradually but I think it is a mistake to attempt to force this. Individuality is one of the cornerstones of creative art and, in the end, should be your aim. However, do not rule out copying at the beginning. Many great artists have spent long apprenticeships copying the work of previous masters and there is no reason why you should not do likewise.

This chapter has been divided into three sections:

Simple exercises to familiarise you with working and casting in relief.

Modelling and casting fruit or other fresh produce.

Design and modelling of abstract work.

I will be taking you on to modelling a human torso in relief in Chapter 7.

Simple Exercises

I would not want you to spend too much time on these exercises – no more than a day – unless they particularly appeal to you. They are very helpful to those with little experience of modelling in clay, and you can produce some very interesting results. However, should you want to get on to something more exciting, do move on to later work. If you are brave enough you may, even, care to tackle next that relief torso in Chapter 7.

I have sketched out some suggestions in Fig. 14, although, as mentioned, I would prefer you to find your own subjects if you can. If you are inclined towards organic subjects then fish, dolphins, birds, fruit and flowers may attract your attention. However, various other subjects can be interesting. 'Man in the Moon', signs of the Zodiac, boats, buildings and Coats of Arms, to name just some, can all be challenging. Coins are particularly interesting. Examine them carefully and you will see that they are beautiful examples of relief work. You cannot work on this scale. The artists for coins work to a substantially bigger scale which is then reduced but you could produce a coin design in a much larger than life scale, say of about 6 inches (15cm) in diameter. Don't bother with the lettering; just do the head or emblem. Keep your eyes open for other subjects, or draw out something of your own, to represent in relief. One great artist wrote, 'It is not the subject which interests me but the way I treat it.' This is well worth always keeping at the back of your mind.

Fig. 14. Suggestions for simple relief figures to be developed on a flat base.

As with most sculpture several different methods, techniques and tools may be employed. As you progress, you will find out which of them suits you best. Experience is essential and now is the time to get it – before you tackle more difficult subjects.

The aim in relief work is not just to produce simple outlines but to develop the surface. Whatever subject you decide upon, keep the modelling fairly shallow to begin with but don't feel too restricted. The main thing is to create an interesting figure and *avoid undercuts*. As mentioned in the last chapter, these will prove troublesome when you come to cast the figures; so, make your relief work well rounded on top with no 'tuck ins' or undercuts.

I must draw attention to another important consideration. Whatever you are modelling, it must dry out evenly.

Uneven drying can cause all manner of trouble later. The problem is that thin parts dry out more quickly than thick parts unless you take steps to prevent this. (The same applies to all modelling work in clay, no matter what the subject.)

If you are going to mould your figure for casting, soon after you have finished it, you need not worry too much. It should remain uniformly moist sufficiently long for the purpose. In this condition it should be firm enough not to distort easily; but neither should any area have become hardened and therefore liable to break off.

However, if there is going to be a pause whilst working, or perhaps some delay before moulding, you must prepare for this.

Good, thick figures are helpful in this respect. Make sure your work is not less than a quarter of an inch (0.5cm) thick at its thinnest point. Cover a figure with a damp cloth if you leave it for any length of time.

A reasonably sure way to avoid thin areas which may dry out is to carve and shape your figure from the top surface of a thick slab of moist clay which you have rolled out and cut roughly to size first. However, this is not always easy because, with all such carving, you have to start at the highest point. A different alternative is to fashion your figure on your work-board first – making sure its bottom will be flat and its contours generally slope towards the outside edge without forming undercuts. Then, gently, lift the figure onto a suitably-sized, fresh slab of clay.

Whichever of these methods you choose, the last step will be to remove excess slab round the edge of your figure. There is no need to follow the edge; if you leave an inch (2.5cm) or so of margin, this will form a nice base for your figure to stand on. It is easiest to make straight cuts so that your base is perhaps square or rectangular but you can decide upon any shape that pleases you.

Alter my suggestions in Fig. 14 if you wish, or think of other ideas. Use your own imagination. I have seen a 'Man in the Moon' with a merry nightcap on his head, for example. However, you must always consider the design, size and method to use, before you begin. If your figures are too small, for instance, they will dry out more quickly and it will be difficult to develop the modelling.

I suggest the following approach – which combines some of the techniques discussed above – as a start. First, roll out a thick slab of clay somewhat larger than your proposed figure. You can now cut out the outline of your figure and then model the features. Or, you can model the features first and then cut out the outline. The advantage of the second method is that you are less likely to lose the shaping that you want. This is because, as you work on features, your clay is almost certain to distort and spread out a little. (Clay does not compress very much and, as you press into it, it has to go somewhere.) However, the effect is less pronounced when you work in the middle of a chunk of clay than when you are modelling close to an edge.

You must remember this in all your future work.

You have to learn what suits you by trial and error and must be guided by your own experience. Sometimes you may want to mix these methods by first doing a little shaping and then cutting out the outline – before going on to modelling finer detail.

The profiles of your figures can be cut out freehand but it may be easier if you mark them out first. There are several ways to mark out a figure:

1.   Make a template out of cardboard, place this on the clay and score round it using a pointed modelling tool, skewer or similar handy item.

2.   'Trace' through a picture of your subject by placing this on the clay and running a pencil or some other

pointed tool lightly along the essential lines. Press just hard enough to leave an impression below.

3.   Place the same picture on the clay and, instead, push a pin repeatedly through the outlines, leaving little pin pricks below. (This is a very old technique used in Portugal for making tiles with relief features on them.)

Once you have your outline clearly defined, it is time to begin to develop the features, bearing in mind at what stage it will be best to remove the unneeded clay slab surrounding your figure which, of course, has to be done at some point. This work is a matter of gentle persuasion and manipulation all round. Whilst I much prefer using my hands for the modelling, you may find sometimes that using small wooden or plastic tools is necessary. Do not attempt too much detail. Just work freely, suggesting the main features first so that you can get them all in the right places and in the right proportions. This should ensure that you will have a good overall figure.

For the 'Man in the Moon', for example, you can introduce contours to the surface by cutting away a little clay using a looped modelling tool or, in some areas, by pressing it into shape. (Remember, though, how it spreads when you press it down.) Then you can model the nose with a small bulbous tip and a smaller one for the nostril. (For this purpose you may need to add a small, half ball of clay, first moistened with water.) The lips can be cut into the underlying clay and the cheeks can be given a 'rounded' appearance. Make sure it all comes together in one smooth, curved surface. However, DO NOT TRY TO DEVELOP THE FEATURES TOO MUCH. It is all too easy to spoil a figure which began simple and good!

For either fish I suggest a figure about 6 inches (15cm) long. Model them with smooth, curved bodies. The fat fish is stylised for fun. Make the body quite plump, falling away towards the tail and head. Scales can be suggested by gently pressing the point of a penknife or similar tool into the surface. It is best to work back from the tip of each scale and overlap them a little. Practice on some spare clay first may help. The two dolphins look more lively when overlapped – which will test your expertise – whilst the sea horse can be made to look its best with slightly craggy features.

The sea horse is a delightful little figure but there are some small problems you need to get round. These affect mainly the tail and the head which, if too thin, will dry out and break off. Again, I would not make this figure less than about 6 inches (15cm) long. It would be best to do so on a good, thick base. Roll out the base first about 8 inches (20cm) by 3 inches (7.5cm). You can apply additional clay for the figure to this base, roughly in the shape for which you are aiming, or, provided your base has sufficient thickness, make a cardboard template of the overall figure first and then apply that to the base. The figure itself wants to be developed in relief not less than half an inch thick (1.25cm) thick at its thinnest parts, building up to a nice, rounded, fat belly. The belly will need extra clay – in a half egg shape. Make sure this all flows smoothly together. Do not worry about any features or detail too early. Wait until you have got a nice overall shape. Then you can consider some detail, if you like. Your sea horse will look quite nice if left smooth; however if you want to add some character, the skin can be made to look quite knurled. There is a long 'spine' running down the body with smaller ridges running out to the edges. You have no need to 'make' these ridges in full; just make shallow indentations with the tip of your little finger along the lines where you want the ridges to be and they will simply occur! There is a thin fin at the back but don't make it too thin. The same applies to the snout. The eye can be a small ball of clay, firmly fixed, or you could just make an indention with the end of a pencil. (It would be useful to look at a picture or two; and a visit to the library might be worthwhile if you wish to go further on detail than this.) If you round off the corners of the base, your sea horse will make a handsome wall plaque. (I explain how to make hanging a plaque easy at the top of page 95.) I usually round them off by laying on the top a coin (or something else round to fit the size) and cut round it.

You can leave all these figures just as they are and make one piece moulds quite satisfactorily. Or, for any which you have not modelled to include a suitable base on which to stand, or which are not really very thick overall, you can position each one on top of its own larger slab of clay, so as to provide it with an individual base. A little undulation, or texture, on the surface of a base adds interest and remember that simply having a base will help to retain moisture and prevent the extremities from drying out and breaking off.

Keep this principle in mind for your future work.

You can make your moulds for these relief figures without a retaining wall, as long as you do not let the plaster spread out too much. Refer to Chapter 4 for the instructions. Being quite small these moulds will not take very long to dry completely. When they are dry – you can lift them off. You may have to slip a table knife, or your clay cutter, underneath first to release the suction. If any clay comes away in a mould do not worry. It will be the casts you want to keep rather than clay originals. Remove the remaining clay figure(s) from your work-board for keeping in an air-tight plastic box. The clay will be good for further use. If there are any pieces of plaster stuck in it, they can be removed later.

Chapter 4 also takes you through the whole casting process appropriate with one piece moulds such as these, step by step.

You can cast your final figures with or without their

bases. If you want to cast one alone – without its base – then only fill in the modelled part when you pour in the plaster for the cast. Otherwise fill the whole mould.

Here is a good extra tip. If you are likely to want to mount your figure vertically or hang it as a wall plaque, insert a small, flat piece of wood into the cast plaster at what will be the back of the figure, before it dries. You then have something to screw into for hanging.

Should you wish to colour some of these pieces of work you can use any of the methods suggested at the end of Chapter 4.

Modelling Fruit or Vegetables in Relief

It is a good idea, first, to make some moulds from real produce. This is helpful because, provided what you choose is hard rather than over-ripe, this will be more rigid and easier to handle than would be a clay model. The items when cast will be superbly accurate.

Apple

Take an apple. As we saw in Chapter 4, if you cut it in half in line with its core and lay one half, cut surface down, on your work-board, you will find you have an indentation – and potential undercut – where the stalk enters. You can deal with this by filling it in with some clay before the moulding, or you can avoid it by slicing your apple in half the other way – at right angles to its core. If you decide to mould the half bearing the stalk on top, just remove it and pour the plaster over. This mould should lift without trouble.

Now try moulding and casting other real fruits or vegetables, anticipating the problems and finding ways to overcome them. One of the most interesting and 'sculptural' fruits is the large red or green pepper. They have lovely flowing curves rolling into each other. A section cut lengthways through one will provide interesting and helpful experience.

Mushroom

For example, take a nice, large mushroom and cut it 'vertically' in half, including down the stem. Place the flat, cut surface of the mushroom on your work-board. If you wanted to mould and then cast this, you would have to fill in the undercut below the cap with soft clay. You can then make some radial scores, if you like, to resemble the 'gills'. This is not 'exactly' like the mushroom but our task, as sculptors, is not always to copy exactly but to interpret faithfully. By 'faithfully', I mean being faithful to our task and to our medium. You may say this is 'poetic licence' but remember from earlier, 'It is not the subject that interests me but the way I treat it.' Creativity lies not just in copying but also in creating new images. You will have no difficulty in making a mould and lifting it, before casting your modelled mushroom.

A small collection of modelled fruits can look very fine assembled in relief on a clay base. Use 'scratch and dab' to fix each item firmly down in an interesting juxtaposition to its fellows. Mould and cast the whole piece if you wish.

After you have cast from some real fruit or vegetables, you can model some others in clay first, bearing in mind you are working in relief, not in the full, three dimensions. Then make a mould of your model and cast in that.

I must mention here that for much of the work described in this chapter, I like to work at a shallow angle. This means propping up your work-board but the arrangement must be rigid. A few books placed behind the board will not be satisfactory. You may be able to make a small, table-top 'easel' at home from two pieces of chipboard hinged together in two places, with a strut fixed at each end to define and fix the angle. Your easel stands on one piece; the struts holding up the other. You will have to determine which angle suits you best.

Abstract Work

The twentieth century artist and sculptor, Ben Nicholson, did a great deal of work in this area and it is worthwhile examining his work and ideas. (Fig. 15 represents an example.)

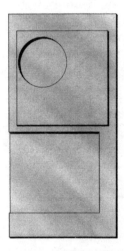

Fig. 15. Drawing from Ben Nicholson abstract.

You could start by making a good-sized clay base about 12 x 8 inches (30 x 20cm) and not less than 1 inch (2.5cm) thick. Then, from other slabs of clay, some thicker, some thinner, cut out a variety of geometric shapes; make triangles, squares, rectangles, circles, preferably of different sizes. Attach these to your base by 'scratch and dab'. By thoughtful arrangement of the shapes, you can make your overall design most interesting. Place some adjacent to others and some overlapping, or perhaps contained within each other.

You will soon discover the problems of overlapping and different levels. Overlaps will have to be filled in below in order to avoid undercuts and produce a finished surface which will be easy to cast.

It is a good idea to make templates for your shapes, cut with a Stanley knife from stiff cardboard. I think it adds considerably to the final result if these shapes are made with great care and accuracy. There are times in sculpture when free activity is called for – which most people enjoy – but at other times a really outstanding result depends upon accuracy and precision.

You might also experiment on a thick clay base with an **Intaglio** effect. Similar cut shapes, or any others you may find, such as the shapes children 'post' through holes in matching outlines, can (provided they are made of hard material) be pressed into a clay base, thus reproducing their shapes below the surface. These hard shapes are then removed, leaving their outlines impressed below the surface. Put a little cooking oil on each shape before you press it into the clay. This will make them easier to pull out without tearing the edges of the clay.

You could even combine, say, **Mezzo** with **Intaglio** relief, and have shapes both below and above the background surface. The main thing is to experiment and develop your own ideas. For a good, dramatic effect, aim for a design which casts interesting shadows. These designs when cast in plaster make very interesting wall plaques. Ben Nicholson usually left his reliefs white, which I find is very dramatic because this accentuates the shadows.

Fig. 16 is included here as a splendid example of relief work where the artist has worked in all the levels of relief and used a variety of techniques. This is a brilliant piece of sculpture and worthy of close examination.

Fig. 16. Pre-Raphaelite relief.

Chapter 6:

Modelling Small Figures

We will now move on to making small figures in three dimensions. This is very interesting and exciting work. First, I shall explain some preliminary considerations and reasons for my suggestions.

If you follow the approach I am putting forward, the figures will not need complicated armatures and most will be easy to cast. However, do not underestimate the potential quality of the work you can do in this area. Probably some of the best sculpture I have done has all been figure work, each piece being under 9 inches (23cm) in length or height. Giacometti, the great Swiss sculptor who lived in Paris, considered that, if he could not carry his work in a taxi, it was too big! Whilst some sculpture, like Henry Moore's outdoor figures, does require greatness in size, it is not essential for most subjects.

Let us consider, again, the material with which we are working – clay. Whilst clay has a relatively poor structural strength, that strength depends both upon the dimensions and construction of the work and on the moisture content of the clay. For example, you could construct a very large cube of clay which would be entirely self supporting. However, if it was excessively wet, it would soon disintegrate into a soggy mess. When modelling without an armature, two rough guides are: (1) that your base must be sufficient to support the height and (2) that the clay must be damp enough to be malleable but firm enough to retain its shape as you model it. Generally, clay is just about right if it does not stick to the hands. When it is too wet it becomes a 'claggy' nuisance.

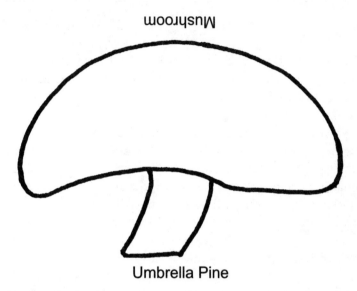

Umbrella Pine

Fig. 17. Umbrella pine.

In Portugal and many southern European countries, there are lovely 'umbrella pine' trees – providing wonderful shade for picnics and grape pickers' siestas. An umbrella pine, when modelled, is inherently top-heavy and unstable unless you are able to provide well-anchored internal support. However, if you turned it upside down, it would resemble a mushroom, and a model of that, resting on its head (stalk upward), would remain stable and stand freely without support (see Fig. 17). This not only tells us something about structure but also about 'stability'. It is as well to remember that all your work *must* be stable. Standing figures, particularly, will otherwise fall over.

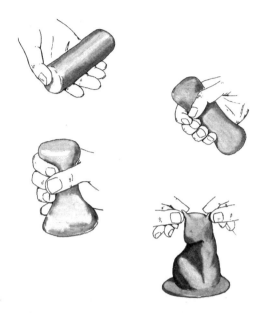

Fig. 18. Cat.

So when you are modelling figures without armatures, they must have a good, firm base which will not only support the height but also ensure stability. It is impossible to give a precise or universal ratio of height to base that is required. This, as mentioned already, will much depend upon the structure of the subject and the condition of the clay. Sculpture, being an art, depends upon having a good 'eye' and 'feel' for your subject. You will develop these as you gain experience and experiment a little; and they will serve as your guide to stability in a figure.

Unfortunately, the human figure does not lend itself to being modelled without support. In a standing figure the ankles are too slim and slender, and extended arms and legs need supporting. However, these characteristics are, happily, quite easy to overcome as you will see.

I suggest proceeding in three stages:

Simple figure work

Elementary human figures

More advanced human figures.

Simple Figure Work

Here are two excellent, simple figures, originally sculpted by Herbert Sanders. The illustrations for these are largely self explanatory.

The first one, in Fig. 18, is a charming little figure, free from fussy detail. From a cylinder of clay which you have squeezed around the middle, make a flat base for the body by striking that part squarely down onto your work-board. Fashion the head and body features with your fingers. This figure could be cast in a two piece mould.

The second one, in Fig. 19, is made from short lengths of clay rolled out to about ⅝ of an inch (1.5cm) diameter, i.e. thickness. The body and legs consist of two equal lengths of this clay joined side by side and bent into position. It will suffice to make the join between them good if you just damp the adjacent edges before pressing them together. The neck, head and tail can be modelled from a little more clay, individually, and added securely using 'scratch and dab'. This little figure would be difficult to cast in plaster and, thus, if you wish to keep it, best fired in a kiln.

Procedures are not given for the next two examples but you should be able to work them out quite easily. Fig. 20, a piece by Betty Locke, is a marvellous example of simplicity and strength whilst retaining charm and elegance. Notice that the surface has been left quite rough. As this one is not easy to cast in plaster, it is best modelled in a clay like

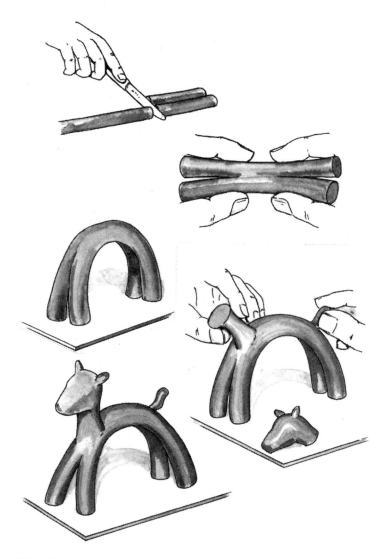

Fig. 19. Pony.

Fig. 20. Girl.

Potclays 1114 Craft Crank which will harden well. Fig. 21 shows my sleeping cat, which was very interesting to do as it curled up into a nice round ball with graceful lines.

You may now care to consider other figures of your choice. Do not attempt to be too realistic. Stylise them into graceful forms without too much detail. It is difficult to model standing quadrupeds without making complicated armatures so, at this stage, it is best to avoid them. Try modelling a pet hamster, dog or your cat whilst it sleeps. (Take a couple of photographs, if you can.) Birds are lovely and sculptural. Penguins, owls and doves are not too difficult, especially if you keep them simple and graceful. Search for pictures from which to work or take photographs.

Elementary Human Figures

Your objective is to model simple, natural figures which do not require intricate work or supporting armatures. These small figures, often referred to as **maquettes**, can be most successful subjects and are popular.

Fig. 21. Sleeping cat.

Reclining Figures

These usually fit in with the above objective. All the figures shown were modelled from friends sunbathing in Portugal. I took several photographs and then worked from these, modifying or changing them to suit my purpose – especially keeping in mind simplicity when casting.

I draped a towel over the first figure, Lilia, in Figs. 22(a) and 22(b), which was not in the original photograph. This reduced the amount of finicky modelling and made casting easier. I like draped figures because you can suggest contours perfectly well, and avoid going into so much detail. However, you have to be equally concerned with the anatomy if your figure is going to be convincing. The drapes must follow, and adhere to the form concealed below. (A cautionary word about anatomy needs to be

Fig. 22(a). Lilia left.

added here. I always tell my students that anatomy does *not* have to be absolutely correct. However, *it must be convincing*.)

To prevent drying out, I modelled Lilia on a good base of clay. To make this figure a little more dynamic, I allowed the draped towel to run down, over one side of the base. I attached her upper arms to the body of the figure, then ran her forearms below the towel on one side and attached to the base on the other – all of this being so as to avoid detail and undercuts and to ease casting. Her legs are joined throughout and I overlapped her feet as I thought they were particularly vulnerable to dryness and even falling off. Keep an eye on this sort of area and make sure it stays moist by occasionally spraying with a fine mist of water. To support the head, I rested it on cushions and let the hair fall back.

Fig. 22(b). Lilia right.

This not only adds grace to a figure but also strength. The head, neck, cushions and hair were thus modelled together – with no undercuts. The whole figure being a single, solid mass of clay made it easier both to work and, ultimately, to cast.

Fig. 23(a). Menina front.

Another similar figure is Menina (Portuguese for a young girl), seen from two angles in Figs. 23(a) and 23(b). Here, I used the same technique again with the head, by resting it on a small pile of rocks. I let the hair fall back so as to hide the folded arms and hands underneath it. We often sit like this when we want to view the scenery. I always try to make these figures look quite natural and relaxed, whilst avoiding minute detail. I raised her right leg to make a more interesting pose but, to avoid undercuts and any need for an internal support, I supported this leg with 'sand and rocks'. (I will draw your attention to Menina's left foot. I joined her feet together to prevent drying out; however, when it came to the casting, her left foot got flattened a little. You don't notice this very much but, I'm afraid, this sort of thing does sometimes happen – so be prepared for it occasionally.)

Fig. 23(b). Menina back.

My third reclining figure (Fig. 24) was Vicky. The same technique was employed with the arms but, with Vicky, I wanted to have her head held erect. I therefore inserted a length of armature wire, well into the body. This aluminium, square section wire (sold in specialist shops) is very malleable and can easily be bent. However, it must be held rigid in the figure. If you use a single strand, make a loop on the end for the head, and bend it a little to get the right pose, before inserting. Should this become loose in the body for any reason, make sure it is packed tight again before proceeding; these supports must be quite rigid. It is often a good idea to make a narrow, U-shaped, 'hairpin' and insert both legs of the hairpin into the clay. This way gives it extra rigidity.

Fig. 24. Vicky.

Small Standing Figures

A simple standing figure can sometimes be modelled without any internal support, as long as you do not attempt to model the legs. These can be covered in a long skirt or gown. If you cloak the head in a hood or shawl this will add strength and support there, by avoiding thinness at the neck level.

As a start, look at the small figure of the pregnant girl, Nascença, in Fig. 25. You might like to try a copy of her. She is only 6 inches (15cm) high in my sculpture, which I mounted on polished stone. As this figure was made from memory to demonstrate making a small maquette without support, I did not include the legs. The arms are joined to the body to obviate armatures but they also suggest tenderness and support. The forward bend of the head, equally, reflects this and helped support the head without an internal armature. The figure was modelled in Potclays 1114 Craft Crank and this set quite hard without cracking or breaking.

Fig. 25. Nascença.

Should you find the head a bit unsteady, insert a short length of armature wire. Whilst this head support needs to protrude only about half an inch (1.25cm) it must be inserted deeper into the body, about three-quarters to one inch (2–2.5cm) to give rigidity.

More Advanced Human Figures

Full Standing Figure

Whilst you may enjoy making other similar, small standing figures, I would like you now – for the purpose of this book – to take a big step forward to modelling a full, standing figure in clay. I suggest a figure about 8 inches (20cm) high. Much more detail is called for and we shall definitely have to introduce a means of support (or simple armature), in order to support the weak structural strength of the clay.

Start by arranging a central support for the whole figure. So long as your figure is not very large, this is no problem. You need a single, fairly strong, metal rod, sticking up through the centre of a piece of wood. You must give some thought to fixing this rod and ensuring that your wooden base is waterproof and will not twist, bend or warp. If you have a thick piece of white-faced chipboard, similar to your work-board, there is no need to treat it. However, if you have plywood – which happens to be very good for this purpose – you will need to give it two or three coats of varnish first. (Be wary of plain softwood as it tends to twist and warp.) Your wooden base needs to be about 6-7 inches (15-18cm) wide. Now find a metal rod. For a figure of about 8 inches (20cm), a 6 inch (15cm) nail would be suitable or you may find a long screw instead. This can be driven (or screwed) through the base from below but you must countersink a recess for its head or your base will wobble about. You must also make certain that it is a very tight fit through the wood and quite vertical. The best way is to drill a hole first, being one slightly less in diameter than your nail or screw. Then you can hammer your nail or tighten your screw, through, and it should be held satisfactorily. Stiff curtain rail, or coat hanger wire, is also a possible alternative but you must ensure it will remain rigid. Hunt around and you may find all sorts of bits of metal which can suit your purpose. Thin threaded rod is excellent with a nut either side of the base, which – for this to work – has to be thick enough to contain the lower nut within a recess.

It is difficult to prescribe a length or thickness for the metal rod because this may depend upon what you can find. If your metal of choice is quite thin and strong, you may decide to run it through to the neck and to support the head but, if it is thicker, you will have to stop short of the head and it may be necessary to insert another, thinner, piece of metal to support that. In general, the central support wants to be not less than about three-quarters of the total height of your figure.

Now, build up your clay around this central support, compressing it firmly together.

I mentioned earlier that the human figure does not lend itself well to modelling in clay because of the narrowness of the ankles. Although you have a nice strong central support, the ankles will still need additional clay. The reason for this is that, with a small figure, the central supporting rod will not allow much clay around it for modelling. That clay is therefore prone to dry out, crack and break away. So this problem must be overcome.

Fig. 26. Susan.

With Susan, in Fig. 26, one arm is attached to the body and holding a bathing wrap which intentionally winds around the bottom of her legs and feet. She is also standing on a rock or mound. All this is modelled in one and gives great support to the ankles and the figure.

The other arm is tucked behind her back, once more eliminating the need for any separate armature, and her hair falls down her back, helping to support her head. If necessary, you could insert a 'hairpin' armature wire for additional head support but Susan stands well with just the central, vertical armature which I used.

My next figure, Michelle, in Fig. 27, was a maquette for a full-size commission and I was asked to show her legs below her skirt. I put a good thick wad of clay behind her legs and scratched this to look like grass. (Michelle spends a lot of time with horses in meadows, so this was quite successful and acceptable to the client.) Nevertheless, I raised her arms and folded them above her head to make one solid mass. To add interest to this figure I modelled Michelle's body and her dress, particularly at the top and back, so that you cannot tell where the dress actually begins. I thought this would add something a little intangible and doing so enabled me to do quite a lot of finer modelling on the back and shoulders. I did the maquette in Plasticine, the life-size model in clay, and the cast, as this was a commission, in resin – about which I say a little more below.

If you want to make permanent figures such as these maquettes, they are best cast in a two piece mould.

Some of my figures in this chapter were cast in bronze-impregnated resin, using silicon rubber moulds. I do not propose to go into this process in this book but I thought you should know of it. These materials, and an excellent little pamphlet on the subject, are available from Tiranti's (see Appendix) for those who might be interested. (The Michelle maquette would look very good cast in plaster – but would not have the professional finish suitable for sale or commission.)

Fig. 27. Michelle.

Chapter 7:

The Human Figure

The female figure has attracted the attention of artists ever since art has been recorded. In fact the very first figure ever found, the Venus of Willendorf, circa 30,000-25,000 BC, was of a woman. (See Fig. 28.) It may be true that in the earliest civilisations such attention was a form of sexual worship or adulation. In both Greek and Roman society the worship of goddesses was common.

In more recent times, sculptors have turned to the female figure not only because of the sexual connotations but because of the lovely shapes and contours gently running into each other, the contrasting forms and the constantly changing shape and mood. Henry Moore likened the female figure to a landscape. Whatever its past fascination, the female figure still seems to hold the ultimate challenge to which most artists turn, and you may find the same compulsion.

I suggest you start this work with a fairly simple, conventional pose in relief, mainly because, in this way, you will most easily learn the essence of the subject. I delve into considerable detail, including the anatomy, because this should serve you well both now and in the longer term.

The Torso in Relief

I have divided the chapter between, firstly, a simple torso in relief and, secondly, a full figure torso, based upon that

Fig. 28. Venus of Willendorf.

relief. My reasons were fourfold:

1. To model a complete figure in three dimensions would require building a more complicated armature, which falls beyond the scope of this book.

2. Working on a torso in relief first gives you an opportunity to get familiar with the overall structure of the human body, its proportions and dynamic poses, with much less complication.

3. Your finished torso in relief will also be much easier to cast than a fully three-dimensional figure.

4. Your efforts later, on the full torso, will be rewarded with greater skills and competence working in clay.

Here are some useful *rough* proportions for the human body. Always check your subject for minor differences:

Fig. 29. Relief torso front.

Overall height standing = 7 x height of head held upright.

Crutch lies half-way between top of head and toes.

Hand = face = foot.

Relaxed arms at the sides when standing have wrists level with crutch fork, elbows with waist.

Breasts are two heads below chin.

Top of pubic hair to sternum = distance from same level to knee.

Inner ankle bone is higher than outer bone.

The pit of the neck is vertically above the centre of gravity (normally passing through the main supporting ankle).

Breasts and shoulders are roughly in line and – on a torso – at an equal and opposite angle (if any) when compared to a horizontal line through both hips (see Fig. 30).

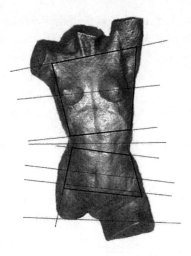

Fig. 30. Torso angles.

I made the complete relief torso shown by Fig. 29. This picture can serve as a basis for your *relief* torso. However, you can use instead any other figure you may prefer. The principles will be the same. My figure is about 14 inches (35cm) high, including the stretched up arms. The lower half, the *pelvic block*, from the bottom of the *pubis* to the top of the hip bones, is about 5½ inches (13.5cm). From there to the pit of the neck, where the collar bones – the *clavicles* – meet, known as the *thoracic block*, is much the same distance.

For your relief torso please look at Fig. 30 again. You begin by placing two thick slabs of clay – normal modelling clay will do – not less than 2 inches (5cm) thick and adjacent to each other, with a roughly triangular gap between them coming more or less in the centre of your work-board. These slabs want to be trapeziform in profile as shown. When you prepare them make sure you drive out any air pockets as with previous work. In this pose the two righthand sides of the body (considered as if you were the model) come closer together. Start with the approximate measurements given below for each slab and allow for the lefthand sides of the body to be roughly 3½ inches (9cm) apart. The triangular gap between the slabs can vary, of course, as in life, by quite a lot. Its main purpose is so that you will achieve a more dynamic pose.

For a female figure the lower slab wants to be about 6 inches (15cm) wide at the bottom and 4½ inches (11.5cm) wide at the top. The upper slab should be about 4 inches (10cm) wide at the bottom and 4¾ inches (12cm) from side to side at the top. The lines I have drawn onto Fig. 30 are indicative of these spatial relationships of the major body areas, rather than precise reflections of the measures I have given.

The upper slab is going to become the rib cage, or upper torso, and the bottom slab the lower torso. You will need to leave a space around your figure of not less than 2 inches (5cm) away from it, for casting – allow more if possible.

Start to visualise your ultimate figure from the beginning so that the size and proportions of the slabs roughly represent the torso – but don't worry unduly about accuracy yet. (In the male, the shoulders are wider than the hips, whereas, in the female, the hips are wider than the shoulders.)

Model both slabs roughly barrel-shapen with each top surface flattened a little more than its curved sides. Now fill in the gap between your two 'halves', joining the clay smoothly into both sections – again, keeping watch that no pockets of air could be formed anywhere.

Next consider the upper body of the torso so that you can take it a stage further. The rib cage is made up of 12 pairs of bones. The top 5 pairs are joined directly to the central 'chest bone' or *sternum*, which, itself, curves gently backwards to the pit of the neck. The rest fall away to the side like wings. Between these 'wings' are the tummy muscles.

Begin to identify these shapes. Pick out the front edge of the wings of the rib cage; start to suggest the tummy; curve the central sternum back as it rises toward the pit of the neck. You will have to add or remove clay according to the demand. (Use a looped modelling tool to remove clay.) Keep damp those areas where you are not working with a very fine mist from your flower-spray from time to time, if necessary. You may want them to remain workable for quite a while. (When leaving the model, cover it with a damp cloth.)

At each top corner of the upper torso, add a suitably thick roll of clay, for the shoulders and arms. Model them only roughly for the time being, adding more clay as necessary. Notice that the left arm is stretched up more vertically than the right arm, which is tilted slightly forward. If we modelled the figure in full, the elbow of the left arm would be above the shoulder; the right elbow would be a little forward of the shoulder, and the arms would be folded above the head. Imagining these positions will help you form the arms correctly.

Don't be too fussy. Keep to the general shapes without detail.
Now switch to the lower torso.
It is very important to keep working on the whole subject at the same time.

To concentrate on one area whilst neglecting another is a mistake; if you do, you will soon lose the shape, the rhythm, the sense of proportion and the relationship between the areas. *Do not consider any fine detail* until you have the whole figure under control and to your liking.

Just as the rib cage is the basic structure of the upper torso, so the *pelvis* is the basis of the lower torso. The pelvis is a massive bone structure, not only supporting the whole body but giving the lower torso shape and beauty. It is very roughly a circular, or ovoid, ring with a hollow centre. The upper part has two strong 'projections' (the *iliac crests* or hip bones), the outlines of which are usually visible. Beneath each 'hip bone' is the large ball and socket joint which houses the thigh bone – the *femur*.

Attached to the ball of each thigh bone is a short neck – the *great trochanter*. This is important in sculpture because it projects beyond the pelvis, finalising the shape of the hip. If you model hips as one smooth curve, they are rather dull and lifeless.

So, the need is to develop these projecting bones to give a more vital shape to your figure as you add the final masses of clay, the leg stubs. Treat these with care or they can look quite ungainly. The left leg is 'moving' forward and raised a little. This movement gives extra 'life' to your figure. Shape it carefully and leave the cut-off surface smooth but with slight undulations. Aim for a clean finish to the edges of both stubs. All bones, naturally, remember, are covered with muscle, skin, fat, ligaments, tendons and other tissue, giving the lovely, undulating, smooth lines of the body.

Between the hips rests the belly. The belly is the lower part of a continuous line of muscles from the rib cage down to the pelvis. For the sake of simplicity I shall refer to the upper muscles as the *tummy* and the lower muscles as the *belly*. Start to identify this area. The belly is fuller and more rounded than the tummy. From the top of the belly there is a contour running down and around each side into the lower groin area below, before rising again out over the thigh on each side. Another contour runs from the belly button down the front and gradually inward to the groin below; there it flattens a little as it carries onto the pubis in the centre of the groin. Around the base of the belly these contours all merge together.

Now return again to the upper torso, in particular the arms and shoulders which will require more modelling and, possibly, a little added clay.

The shoulders, remember, are linked by the two collar bones the clavicles, which meet the sternum in the centre and thus form what we describe as the pit of the neck. The clavicles are raised above the surrounding area, making the clavicle bone on either side appear as a graceful ridge. Pick these out carefully. The clavicles are very expressive, especially when seen in relation to the lovely, neck muscle – the *sternocleidomastoid*. This long, strong, usually visible and very 'mobile' muscle, particularly beautiful in women, runs from the pit of the neck to behind the ears. In the torso you need only suggest its beginning. Full face you can see both sides of this muscle but, as the head turns, one side will disappear whilst the other becomes even more prominent. This neck muscle is particularly well-defined in Fig. 44, an African girl.

The breasts are interesting because they have no muscle and, therefore, cannot move, or change shape, of their own accord. You need to consider this most carefully when you model them. Whilst generally equal in size, they only change shape when some other part of the body is moved. If the figure is standing, then the breasts will hang and be fuller than when the same person is lying down on her back. My relief torso is of a standing figure with both arms upstretched. This poise has lifted and tautened the breasts.

So, you must always relate the shape of a breast to the specific pose when you are doing a female figure. That shape will alter almost whenever your subject moves. Such are the main considerations which should enable you to judge how much more clay you may need to form the breasts true to life.

The breast line – the line of the nipples – is roughly half way between the top and the bottom of the rib cage and is *parallel to the shoulders*. The nipples usually point slightly outwards rather than directly to the front. The outer contour of each breast joins the muscles of the respective arm at the shoulder. This happens in one continuous line which should be well defined and which establishes the armpit.

We are now nearing completion and your figure should look something like your objective. You only need to put on the finishing touches and clean up a little. Again, I offer a word of caution: do not overdo your finer modelling. The problem is knowing when to stop. Many a good work has been ruined by endless tinkering about trying to make improvements. A sound principle to remember is: *a work of art should always be finished but never completed.* This is one of the key reasons why you should always keep the whole work going along together. At any stage after all the major parts are in position, you should be able to stop and the work look finished – even if you could go on adding or refining more.

Final Touches

Pick out the edges of the rib wings and smoothly 'round' them off. These are very feminine. In the male they are more hidden by muscle. The nipples may need a little more work on them: for the sake of casting the figure it is best if you can keep them rather small, round and gracefully moulded into the surrounding breasts. Check for a nice shape to the tummy. This should be one long sweeping mass of graceful muscle, bending in line with the upper torso before reaching the more rounded, oval-shaped belly. Make a small indent for the navel, which needs to be in the middle, just below the top of the pelvis. Attend to the pubic region. Be sure it is well tucked in at the base and that the sides between the legs are well defined. Use the end of a modelling tool for this. You can press quite deeply without causing any casting problems. With the pubic hair just model a gentle, wavy surface, keeping it shallow and with no undercuts. Have another look at the leg stubs. Suggest the muscular 'rhythm' of the thighs carefully by hand.

At this stage you should consider obviating any undercuts around the whole figure. If you want to cast your figure in a one piece mould you may have trouble with the potential undercuts in the armpits above and alongside the breasts. If so, it would be best to use a waste mould. However, if you prefer to cast in a one piece mould, keep the armpits shallow and reduce the breasts – making them more like those of a young girl or of a woman lying back at rest – and run them, smoothly, in to the chest so that any potential undercut is avoided.

Preparing for Moulding

You can achieve a nice smooth, clay figure by 'polishing' the surface with your dampened fingers and thumb. This smoothness becomes a benefit a little later when you come to remove your final cast from its mould; it helps prevent the two plasters getting locked together. You may find it an advantage to wipe over the surface, first, with a small sponge. A light delicate touch is called for. For this I have found real sponge is best. Plastic sponges are too coarse and not resilient enough; whereas a natural sponge is easier to use softly, bounces back and remains quite resilient. Keep your sponge clean by constantly rinsing it out in water and squeezing it almost dry. You can buy small, natural sponges in art shops and chemists.

A wooden modelling tool may help with this smoothing process where space is restricted. You should need only a tiny amount of moisture as you proceed – so be careful not to add too much. Just dip the fingers, or the tool, in clean water. An alternative to using water is to use a very meagre amount of cooking oil. This can also assist release of your mould.

Making the Mould and Casting

Chapter 4 sets out exactly how to do this one piece mould. However, some extra tips may come in useful. As this is quite a large figure it may be easier, when removing your clay torso from its mould, to turn the whole thing, *including* your work-board, upside down first. Then remove the work-board by slightly twisting it. When you come to the removal of your cast from that mould it may require a little more patience. Assuming it is 'upside down', reverse it again first. Provided you did use release agent quite liberally you should not have any difficulty. Most often the cast, with a gentle tap, just drops out. If it does not come away easily, try more gentle tapping or pour over some hot water, as suggested in Chapter 4. If all else fails, you may have to chip it off, like a waste mould, but this should not be necessary. Patience and care are the main imperatives.

You can colour your relief torso if you wish, using one of the methods suggested at the end of Chapter 4. Otherwise a nice sheen on the surface will alone enhance the contours of this figure. Apply this using a soft, white wax polish which will buff up nicely.

The Full Figure Torso in Three Dimensions

This is probably where many readers would have liked to start! However, I feel sure that those who have worked carefully through the earlier exercises will have been rewarded. We have, after all, packed two or three years of full-time study into this book so far. Now, you will begin to benefit from this experience and I feel sure your work will be richer and better for it.

Before you start this full torso there are one or two additional considerations for you to take into account. It will be too late when your figure is completed. You must consider the sort of clay to use, whether or not to use a central support for the figure and what sort of finish you would like. It is now that you will find that a turntable is useful – see Chapter 2.

The most suitable clay will depend upon what you propose to do when you have finished the figure. If you intend to leave it to dry out as it is, then the best clay with which I am familiar would be the Potclays 1114 Craft Crank, and it would be worth your while getting a bag. Fig. 31 was modelled in this clay some years ago and has remained in excellent condition ever since. If you intend to cast your figure, then ordinary modelling clay will be satisfactory. You may also like to consider the type of finish you prefer. If you want a rougher, textured finish, which is very interesting, then 1114 is the clay but, if you prefer a smoother finish, you must go for a normal, modelling clay.

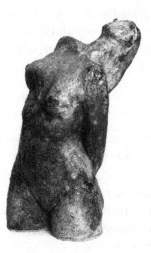

Fig. 31. Lilia torso.

Similar considerations apply to whether or not you use a central support. Again, this depends to some extent upon what you want to do with the torso when you have it finished. A torso of this size (we will use dimensions from the relief torso earlier) can be modelled without any support at all – as some of mine were. The disadvantage is that there then is always a chance of it getting knocked over, or of it falling off any base you may have given it. Were it to break badly it could then be lost forever. I nearly always find, in any event, and for a whole variety of reasons, that I have to move a figure at some point during the modelling; very often I then discover that the underneath has dried out first. If there is no central support this makes the waist and the upper half rather vulnerable. So, in turn, I'm forced to rely on some poor soul to hold the body of the figure steady whilst I lift the whole piece, still secure on my work-board, to move it wherever necessary. It is to avoid such 'nightmares' that I do recommend, here, the use of a central support – albeit a simple one. Having said that, it is worth mentioning that, if you intend to leave your full torso to dry out for keeping in its clay form, it would be best to remove the central support first. There's a simple way to make this possible: before you start creating the pelvic block, cover the *support* with a thin plastic bag. Wrap this lightly around the full height of your support pillar, so that it will easily slip off – lengthwise – when you want to slide the support out from the inside. This removal has to be done with great care whilst the inside clay is still damp. There is a risk of some damage to the outside whilst you part your figure from its support; however, as long as the outside is also still a little damp, some remedial work can usually be carried out afterwards.

If you propose to cast this torso, it lends itself to having moulds made vertically rather than horizontally. Having a central support is then highly advantageous as it holds the figure steady whilst you apply the separating wall and the plaster for the mould. (Incidentally, there is no fear of this figure slipping down the central support as long as it is standing firm on the wooden base into which your support has been fixed tightly.)

So, give some thought to all these matters *before* you start.

This is a fairly large and quite heavy, full torso. Therefore, how you position and work the clay is important. You must ensure that the figure becomes, as you progress, a single, solid mass of clay. Any gaps of air between applied wads of clay may prove disastrous as the figure dries out. (Whenever I have seen cracks appearing in such figures as these – which have often baffled the worker – I have dug out around the crack only to find that there was a pocket of air beneath it so that the layer of clay around the air pocket was thinner than the rest.) I have to tell you that it is very difficult to fill in such cracks satisfactorily when they occur, even if the clay is still damp. For all these reasons, whenever I apply wads of clay to build up mass, I always 'bash' it together, either with my fist or a sturdy piece of wood – often my rolling pin – until I feel pretty sure there is no danger of any air having been contained within.

I suggest you make your full, three-dimensional torso of the same relief figure I gave you in the last exercise. You will be familiar with the front of this figure and will have discovered some of the problems and how to overcome them. Now you are going to model the same figure together with its back portion, as shown in Fig. 32.

Begin with the pelvic block and then build up two good, slightly oversize diameter cylinders, one for each leg stub. These leg stubs must be firmly attached to the pelvic block so that all three parts become a single mass. You may need extra clay where the legs join the trunk.

You start the pelvic block by making a suitable rectangular *block* of clay around a simple central support. (How to make this support, tightly held by a wooden base, was explained in the last chapter.) Make sure that the size of the

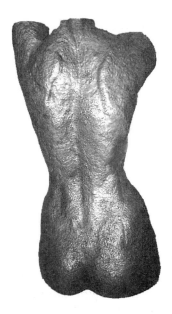

Fig. 32. Relief torso back.

wooden base of your support stand exceeds, by at least 2 inches (5cm) all round, that of your figure. Position the legs you have made roughly in place on the wooden base holding your central support. They will help carry the extra weight as you build up the pelvic block. Now pack wads of clay together to create the basic shape pelvic block and 'finish' its top at a slight angle as indicated by Fig. 30.

This angle (as explained for making the relief torso earlier) will provide your figure with the vitality of apparent movement. For the moment (if you are doing the same torso as mine), your block needs to slope a little on the top from the right side of the body to the left, whilst being quite level all across that slope from front to rear.

Don't model the legs finally yet: all you wish is to ensure that the joins with the body are smooth and firm.

The pelvic block wants to be not less than about 7 inches

(17.5cm) wide, 5 inches (12cm) thick and 6 inches (15cm) high. These measurements are not critical and, if you are modelling a different size figure, you will have to use your judgment. At this stage you are only concerned with getting the required masses of clay together and in place for modelling and carving later.

On top of the pelvic block, you are going to model another of which the bottom will finish at a similar angle but tilted in the opposite direction. (Look at Fig. 30 again.) This, thoracic, block should be mainly narrower, taller and not so thick – say 6 inches (15cm) wide by 7 inches (18cm) high and 4 inches (10cm) thick. Wedge enough clay in the gap between your two blocks to support the upper body one at the angle you want, whilst you are forming it to the right overall shape. You must use your eye as you proceed so as to see that it begins to look 'right' but you must also leave all detailed modelling until later. There's a lot else to do first.

As soon as practicable fill in completely between the blocks where you have made your angle. Make sure this extra clay is well pushed in to avoid air pockets. Model the area a little as you go, to form the waist, and to ensure that this joining of the thoracic block to the pelvic block securely merges the whole figure, as far as possible, into a single, homogenous mass. Remember to use your spray mist if signs of drying too quickly become evident.

The next three forms cannot be added as pre-made cylinders – or they are likely to fall off. Because of the stage you have already reached, they must instead be built up strongly *in situ* from small wads of clay firmly pressed together. I refer to the arms and the neck. The right arm should be quite short and stubby, or it will need extra support. For the neck, just build a solid cylindrical mass between the arms for the moment.

You need two roughly-shaped mounds for the breasts. Make sure the additional clay for these is strongly attached to the main body. The clay for the breasts themselves should be quite firm. This firmness will be important when you come to model them to their finished shapes.

By this time you should have a quite good, outline figure. If any major 'surgery' still strikes you as essential, *do it now*.

From this point, now that you have the main masses of clay in place, you can begin modelling important outlines. With sculpture it is usual to start at the highest point and work downwards. However, for the back of this clay torso, I would start lower down, in the middle of the back at waist level, and work out and up (as well as further down) from there. I think the back is often rather neglected but, in fact, it is rather lovely, with lots of small, undulating ripples of muscle. The spine is set in a lovely 'valley' with firm, rounded muscles either side. Try to suggest these muscles accurately, if generally. This is a truly beautiful area and should be fully developed in your work.

You will probably have to remove some clay near the waist and add some for the buttocks, as well as make similar, smaller, adjustments elsewhere. Removing modest amounts of clay is best done neatly by cutting away with a looped modelling tool. Provided you keep the whole piece reasonably moist with your water spray, this work should all run together smoothly.

Model the buttocks carefully; they are not just round but more oval in shape. The outer sides are slightly flattened and angled outwards from the hips. There is a slight depression on each of those sides, surrounded by muscle. Develop the hips and the great trochanters, adding more clay where necessary.

Now, move higher up the back to develop the triangular shoulder blades, the *scapulae*. Model this area carefully and carry the shaping forward to the shoulders and arms.

Do not attempt to finish off any area at this stage. Just keep it all going until you have a figure which roughly resembles your aim. Look for the proportions and lines being fairly well defined. Try to make sure the upper torso does not look stiff or awkward and that – if anything – it leans back a little. This will add gracefulness and vitality to your work. (You can lean the upper torso back, *a little*, by gentle pressure with both hands and also suggest a twist on the body, to enhance the angle relative to the pelvic area. You must do this with great care and not attempt too much.)

Work further on the arms, neck and the leg stumps. Again, don't attempt to finish them completely just yet but you should be able to define the final shapes. Pay attention to the area between the arms, as well as to the muscles of the shoulders.

On the front of your torso you need to follow the same procedure I set out for the torso in relief with which I started this chapter. Whilst the paragraphs above have concentrated on the back of the figure, in practice you should be developing the front simultaneously. Remember my remarks there about the breasts. If rounded and smooth they will not cause any problems when casting.

When you are reasonably happy – in particular with the all-round impression – it is time to enter the final phase. Return to work on each feature, in turn, which you may feel could do with a little more attention, a little more detail.

Let me repeat though, *DON'T OVERDO IT*. Call a halt sooner rather than too late . . .

Finishing Touches

The torso of Lilia, shown in Fig. 31, was modelled in Potclays 1114 Craft Crank and left as it was with a fairly rough surface. (She was not cast until over a year later when I was asked for an additional copy.)

If you are using a normal modelling clay, you may prefer a

very smooth finish. How to obtain this I have explained already on page 125.

Another excellent finish is to apply small pellets of clay – no bigger than peas – pressed close together against the surface of the figure and then flattened a little with the end of a piece of broomstick. This is a very dramatic finish which seems to add a great deal to a figure. It will not give any trouble when casting.

Making the Mould and Casting

This figure, being 'in the round', requires a mould which can be easily removed. This can be done by using a two piece vertical mould, from which, of course, you can cast more than one figure.

Fig. 33. Torso separation line.

The technique is given in Chapter 4. However, I must add a word or two about placing the separating wall, as this is critical. The separation line (Fig. 33) should run along the sides of the torso, generally following the most prominent points on both sides of the rib cage and both hips. You could start at the right side of the rib cage by scoring a faint line down and over the hip. Then, from where you started, take this line up and across the centre of the right arm stub, across the top of the neck stub and both shoulders. Carry on across the centre of the other arm stub, down the arm, and continue down the left side of the rib cage and over the left hip. When you come to the forward strutting leg stub, carry the line forward across the side of the leg to the edge of the leg stub and then down to the base as shown. The aim is to ensure that you leave nice curves both sides of the line with no undercuts. I did not draw this line in one, almost continuous stroke, as described but first drew shorter lines, where I wanted them to be, across the arm and neck stubs and then along the line of the forward, left leg stub. After that I was able to join them all together in one continuous line. Where the line from the hip joined the line of the left leg, you will notice I drew quite a large graceful curve for the reason given above.

When you have marked your separation line, you must consider what type of partition you are going to use: clay wall or shims. Because the shoulder area between the arms may prove a little difficult, it may be easier to use a clay wall. Follow the instructions in Chapter 4 very carefully. If you are using a clay wall, don't forget to make key holes in the surface facing the side you are going to mould first. (I suggest the front.)

When your partition is ready – begin to flick thin (Mix 1) plaster on to the front surface, making quite sure it goes into every niche and corner. Try to keep the top of your partition clean. This is especially important if using a clay wall; the plaster should not reach over it at any point. Also, for this large figure, keep your wooden base as clean as possible from dropped plaster. When you have applied one thin layer, and are sure the figure is fully covered, add more plaster (now Mix 2) to build up a strong mould, not less than three-quarters of an inch (2cm) deep and a little thicker next to the partition, if possible. (This, you will recall, can prove invaluable if you have to use much strength, or a tool, for separating the two moulds.)

Continue from here exactly as instructed in Chapter 4 right through until you have your cast in front of you.

When your excitement has peaked will be time enough to tidy up the cast and colour and/or polish it if you wish. All the information you need is in Chapter 4.

Chapter 8:

Modelling Faces in Relief

This chapter and the next one are devoted to modelling the face and head. The subject divides well into three stages:

A freehand study in relief

A portrait of a known subject, in relief

A full-size head of a person you know (Chapter 9).

Trying your hand at a freehand face in high relief will enable you to understand and become familiar with the face as a subject; to consider facial proportions and their relation-ships with each other; to develop details; and to discover some of the complications and ways to surmount them before attempting a live portrait.

Having gained some experience you should be ready to repeat the exercise but now working on the face of a person you know. This will be quite demanding and will require taking and working to fairly precise dimensions.

In stage three you will want to model a full-size, complete head of your subject. This will include building a suitable support and working in the full, three dimensions, again to fairly exact parameters.

Before you start let's consider some elementary anatomy and proportions. Every face is different. Some people have large ears, some small; and so it is, likewise, with the nose and mouth. The proportions given below are 'general' and

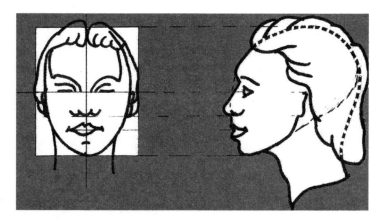

Fig. 34. Face proportions.

approximate but they will help you to get started, so that you can then adjust and refine. The head, as a whole, is shaped rather like an egg with the larger end – *the cranium* – at the top, from where it sweeps down to the more pointed chin. Fig. 34 shows how it is supported – at an angle – by the neck.

Fig. 35 demonstrates the following generalisations:

1.   Looking at the head from the front, the eyes are set about half way between the top of the head – *not the top of the face* – and the bottom of the chin.

2.   The width of each eye and the distance between them are all roughly equal.

3.   The ears are approximately level with the eyes and nose, with their lobes perhaps reaching a little lower.

4.   Each corner of the mouth aligns more or less with the pupil of the eye above.

5.   The inner corner of each eye is about in line with the outside of the nose bulb below.

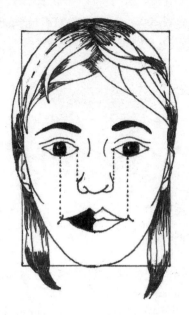

Fig. 35. Face alignment.

These are only rough approximations, satisfactory for a freehand face. When you come to portrait work you must take measurements, be guided by the particular features of your model, and examine closely the relationships between one feature and another.

Modelling a Freehand Face in Relief

Your objective, here, is to work quite freely on any full-sized face which may appeal to you. By full-size, I do not mean you to be too fussy; 'about right' will do. This is only a learning exercise.

You may have a particular face in mind, you might like to look at a picture or photograph, or you may just let your imagination run free. In any event the problems are similar. Figs. 36-39 and several related tables, which follow them, will give you a clear idea of how to navigate the terrain. Consider carefully all the information and directions they include.

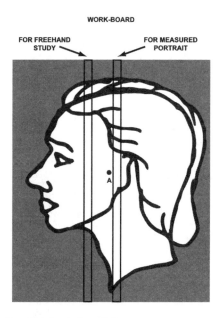

Fig. 36. Depth lines for faces in relief.

You are working in relief on a flat surface but the face and the figuring will be in full depth. So, first, you need to decide how deep your figure is going to be; that is, how far back into the head you are going to work. I suggest you do not include the ears for this first exercise. A line at a depth of about 1 inch (2.5cm) behind the eyes, in front of the ears, would be fine but exactly where is not critical. This cut-off line will equate with the surface of your work-board. All behind it will not be part of your work; all in front you will work in full. Fig. 36 shows two such lines, the left one being suitable for your freehand face in relief.

I like to work on reliefs on a tilted work-board as discussed in Chapter 5, page 96. I am going to assume that, for these faces in relief, your work-board will be of a rectangular, portrait shape rather than square, and large enough to accommodate the face.

In the middle of this work-board draw with a pencil or chalk two straight lines – a horizontal and a vertical one – these being from top to bottom and from one side to the other, crossing at right angles in the centre. The horizontal line, as shown in Fig. 34, will identify for you the line of the eyes. Make certain, as I emphasised before, that *this eye line comes at the centre of the whole head, not just of the face.* This may seem a bit puzzling at first as the very top of the head may not be part of your work.

By looking at both Figs. 34 and 37, you can also mark the extremities of your proposed freehand head directly on your work-board. They are the width between the ears, from **A** to **A**, and the height from the bottom of the chin to the top of the head, **B** to **F** – even though the true position of **F** may come *beyond* your work-board. For each pair, both marks should be equidistant from the centre-point. The edges of my white rectangle in Fig. 34 pass through these marks. Since this is a freehand exercise the overall size of the head is not critical but the bigger it is, the better and easier your task will be. A face about 9½ inches (24cm) tall and 5½ inches (13cm) wide would be fine.

The positions of the cardinal points of the head by the way, shown by Fig. 37, can be described quite accurately as follows:

A – as close to the ear as possible, just in front of the ear cavity; **B** – the base of the chin; **C** – middle of hair line, where the forehead meets the hair; **D** – centre-point of eye line, in recess just above bridge of nose; **E** – tip of nose; **F** – back of head, on skull, beneath the hair.

Your next step is to join up freehand with your chalk or

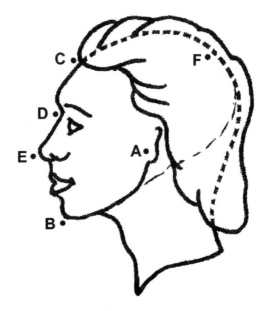

Fig. 37. Cardinal points of the head.

pencil, the outline of the *whole head* – from top to bottom
and from side to side. Your outline must be a nice large egg
shape with the smaller end at the bottom, and this must
relate correctly with the two centre-lines you earlier drew
crossing in the middle. I find it useful to draw in that
rectangle (Fig. 34) first, through the four extremity points,
and then fill in the egg shape within that. This helps me to
balance the drawing and make each side about equal. (I have
marked the rectangle on Fig. 35 also, to give you another fix
on where it should be.)

    Once your work-board is mapped out in this way, you can
start work. Fill in your outline with clay (ordinary modelling clay is fine for this exercise) put on in small handfuls –
making sure they are all well pressed together. Use your fist
or a piece of wood to bang them together, or roll the clay
out with a rolling pin first. The clay wants to be a good inch

(2.5cm) thick. Use a kitchen knife, slightly dampened with cooking oil, to achieve a clean edge to your outline. Slant this edge down each side, inwards a little, suggesting the inward sweep of the sides of the face. Work in a similar but perhaps less pronounced fashion around the top of your figure, and below it, around the chin. Remove any surplus clay off your work-board out of the way.

It is useful now to mark your centre-lines very lightly on top of the clay. You can pick up where they should be from the chalk or pencil marks still visible on your work-board at the edges.

Along the line of the eyes, equidistant from the centre, scoop out two cavities for the eye sockets. I usually do this with my thumbs, as they seem to be about the right size and shape. Having these in place, first, will help you identify where the cheeks, the nose and the forehead should be.

Begin to build up the nose below the eye line. Press on three small balls of clay: two for the nostrils and a slightly larger one for the tip of the nose. Add a little clay for the ridge of the nose and model the whole a little, just enough to 'blend' in and look like the nose for the moment. Add a little clay for the cheeks and run them, smoothly, into the surrounding face, nose and eye sockets.

Don't be too fussy at this stage; you can always remove or add a little clay later. Focus instead on keeping the whole thing balanced and 'together' as you proceed.

(Incidentally, when you add clay to a relief figure like this one, it is not always necessary to use 'scratch and dab' – although this will not do harm. All you need is to dampen both sides to the join a little, either with your flower spray or a small paintbrush. Do not make the clay too wet. Just ensure the attachment surfaces are moist and there is good adhesion.)

You will probably have to add more clay for the forehead. For this, roll out a rectangle of clay about half an inch

(1.25cm) thick; the length and width you can determine to match your freehand face but don't try to be too accurate. Press the extra clay firmly in place and roughly model the forehead.

This slopes back a little and, from the hair line onwards, recedes into the cranium. Somewhere here, of course, it must disappear from your board. The sides of the forehead fall away sharply to form the temples and run on, often with a slight indentation, down into the sides of the face.

Above the nose, between the tops of the two eye sockets, is a small, triangular area running outward and upward before reaching the forehead. If you regard all three as a single area across the face at this level, you can model this as a dip, so that it appears quite consistent and has a minor undulation each side as it passes above each eye. Smooth the upper edge of this dip round into the forehead.

Put a small knob of clay where the chin will be. Model this smoothly into its surroundings.

Now put in the lips. These should join together just about half way between the highest part of the chin and the bottom of the nose – perhaps a little higher. As they protrude a little, put two thin rolls of clay here, tapered towards each end, one for the upper lip, one for the lower. You can put just one thicker roll and shape it later but two rolls better establish the sharp division between the two lips.

However, you must continue to avoid being too fussy about detail for now.

Next, model the eyes. Make two similar, but shorter and thicker, tapered rolls of clay. In the majority of faces the eyes, when open, are pretty equal in size, so I suggest you make them each to the same profile. Fit one into each eye socket. Position them carefully, just above the horizontal line; that is, more or less resting on it, as seen in Fig. 34. The impression that you want is that their pupils, although themselves generally not possible to represent in sculpture, are equidistant from where your horizontal and vertical centre-lines cross.

Add the eyelids. A wafer thin layer of clay above and below each eye will define how much 'white' of each eye is 'seen'. Look again at Fig. 35. Notice that the width of each eye is equal; and that the distance between the inside corners of each pair of eyelids should equal the same width. When forming the eyelids, leave their 'closing' edges nice and crisp – don't worry if they appear to be too thick. Keep your clay moist using a fine mist from your flower spray, so that you can continue to work with it easily. You must also smooth the eyelids where they run into the cheeks, nose, temples and the underside of the forehead.

Check that the ends of the lips are each roughly in line with the pupil of the eye above. You may need to adjust them a little for overall width. Another early-stage task, if you want to show some neck, is to form one, thinly, below the chin and give it a smooth, flat or wavy stub.

Now it's time to stand back for a long, hard look. You should have something roughly resembling the face you envisaged even if it looks rather grotesque here and there. Decide what still needs to be done and you can let yourself go. Start working on the details but still keeping the whole face going along together. *Do not attempt to 'finish' any one feature completely. Keep working away at the whole face, switching in turn from one part to another, improving the overall visage little by little.* I'm sure that gradually you will find that by working along these lines, you establish a really human 'feel' in your freehand relief portrait.

Final Touches

Once you have captured that 'feel', return to the main features – where necessary – to finish off. Here are some tips:

Lips. Work on a nice outline and curve the surface of the lips inwards towards each other. Make this more pro-

nounced in the centre than the edges. Develop a slightly
wavy line in the middle and ensure the lips are level. Slightly
tuck the corners in just below the surface as depicted in Fig.
35. There is a distinct concave indentation above the centre
of the upper lip and going up to the base of the nose. From
behind each nostril to below the cheek on that side, there is
also a quite visible line, usually becoming more conspicuous
with age.

Nostrils. Work on these carefully giving the bulbs a nice
shape. Be sure they are roughly equal and level, and suggest
the nostril cavities but do not go too deep.

Eyes and Eyelids. Work at these carefully and patiently if
you need to do more. Think of the eyeball sector which is
seen, as being rather like a segment of an orange but with
only the outer perimeter on view. Give them both a lovely,
equally rounded shape, tucked well in at the corners. Do not
consider identifying the iris or pupil of the eye. I will refer to
this again in the next chapter. For now just leave the eyes
and their lids as overall shapes formed in the lines I have
described.

Hair. If you need any hair showing, add some clay for it
and comb this back with an ordinary, wide-toothed comb,
or model it in rough, broken waves. You may fall short of
the top head mark or even overrun a little. It largely depends
upon the thickness of hair you would like to see on your
freehand subject. There's no need to stick too rigidly to the
dimensions.

YOU MUST NOW DECIDE WHEN TO STOP.

You need not spend too much time on this face. It is only
intended as an exercise for the next one but one which will
help your understanding considerably when you come to
that.

I suggest you skip moulding and casting this exercise
figure unless you want the practice – which is not a bad idea
– or have other reasons for doing so.

Modelling a Likeness, in Relief, of Someone You Know

This will, probably, be the most demanding work you have attempted so far.

You will need a pair of callipers. These can be bought or you can easily make a pair. These are useful for many jobs and essential for modelling a portrait head of a living person. However, I do not necessarily recommend purchasing a set. Bought sets are often made of metal and usually have sharp points which can be quite dangerous when measuring a face. For this reason, I made a simple set of callipers in wood some years ago, and I have used them regularly ever since.

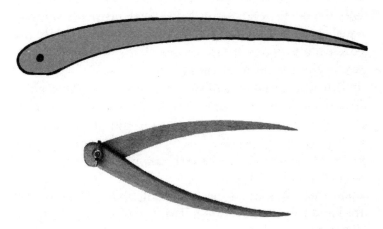

Fig. 38. Callipers.

Cut out two arms, about 11 inches (27cm) long, as shown by Fig. 38, from thin wood – plywood will do. Drill holes as shown. Their diameter is not critical but it must make a tight fit for a small brass nut and bolt. I found a small countersunk bolt screwed through the wood with a finger nut on the other side satisfactory. A small spring washer under the nut is useful as it prevents the nut from coming loose. Clean up the edges of the wood with sandpaper to avoid splinters.

You also need a live model. Perhaps a relation or a friend will oblige. Keep this person involved as much as you can by explaining at all times what you are doing. When my models are not actually sitting, I usually suggest they stand near me whilst I work. Then they can see the work progressing, which they seem to enjoy. You cannot expect anyone to sit still for hours and, in practice, if you proceed along the lines I suggest below, only one or two brief sittings will be necessary.

Begin by taking a few photographs of your subject. These should be taken in a good light as close to the subject as possible. There is an advantage if you can hang a plain, light-coloured cloth behind the subject so that the outlines are quite clear against that background. The key photographs needed are full face (and neck for future reference) and one profile shot from each side.

When you come to sculpting the whole head it may be necessary also to take a photograph of the back of the head, so you might as well do this at the same time. In addition to the key photographs take as many more as you can from all angles. (A top shot from above the temples looking down at an angle is very useful.)

This photography session will enable you and your model to get used to working together; you will get a 'feel' for your subject – the general outlines, contours, hairstyle and the natural way the person's head is held. Try to capture natural poses, character and personality. I believe this is more important and dynamic than a simple image. Quite often, I take some video footage as well. I rove around my subject taking film from as many different positions as I can. I have found this extremely useful. Not only can this be projected larger onto a TV but I frequently capture angles and nuances which I would not, otherwise, have noticed. (Incidentally, I have a

TV and video player set up in my workshop for immediate playback whilst I am at work on the subject of the film.)

For your subject's face, in relief, I suggest you work to a base line which runs behind the cardinal points **A** – and in relation to which you can take your measurements. Figs. 36 and 37 and earlier text in this chapter defined the positions of the cardinal points of the head.

Now, using your callipers, take ALL the measurements set out in the tables below. Just make a numbered list to which you can cross-refer as required. Fig. 39 correlates my item-ised list with lines drawn on a head to help you identify each measurement needed. It is a good idea to mark the cardinal points **A-E** (see Fig. 37 and page 141) on your subject's face with a felt-tip pen having ink that will wash off. In this way you can be sure that all measurements relate to the same parameters.

WIDTH OF FACE

See Figs. 37 and 39.

1   Maximum width: **A** to **A**.

2   Width of forehead.

3a   Maximum distance across both eyes.

3b   Width of single eye = approx. distance between eyes.

4   Width of nose at base.

5a   Width of mouth.

5b   Depth of lips.

6a   Width of neck below chin.

6b   Width of jaw across lips.

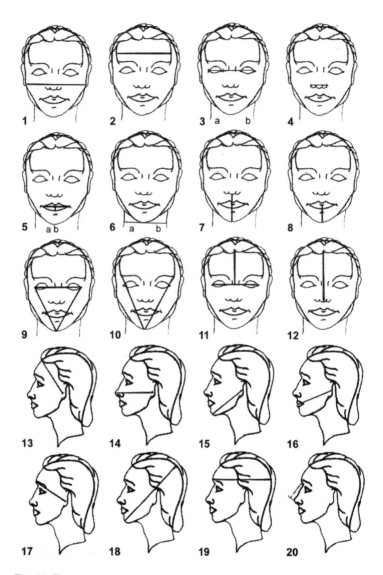

Fig. 39. Face measurements.
This figure can be photocopied and enlarged should you prefer to write your measurements directly onto it.

LENGTH OF FACE

7   Chin to nose: **B** to **E**.

8   Chin to centre of lips.

9   Chin to corners of eyes (both sides). This will help establish the eye line.

10   Chin to corner of each brow above the eyes – if you describe an arc centred on the chin and passing through both these points, its radius would be the length of both these lines (which are the same length).

11   Eye line to hair line: **D** to **C**.

12   Nose to hair line: **E** to **C**.

DEPTH OF HEAD AND FACE IN PROFILE

(Check these from both sides and see that they tally.)

13   **A** to hair line **C**.

14   **A** to tip of nose **E**.

15   **A** to **B**.

16   **A** to centre of lips.

17   **A** to forehead ridge above **D**.

18   Chin **B** to back of head **F**.

19   Depth of head, from forehead ridge horizontally to back of head.

20   Length of nose.

For this measured portrait in relief you should work on the

basis that the surface of your work-board runs just behind the cardinal points A, as in Fig. 36. Bear in mind that the size of its oval – were you doing a full head – would be **B** to **F**. Map out the complete outline of your model, as you did before, in chalk or pencil on the surface of your work-board. Apply the outside measurements you have taken. Include the horizontal and vertical centre-lines, so that you can check everything relates to them properly.

Choose the clay in which you would like this piece of work to be. Any *modelling* clay will do but for other considerations to make about clay, refer back to Chapter 1.

Now fill in your outline with the clay. Put it on in small handfuls pressed well together as previously. Remove surplus clay around the outside of your figure and re-draw your horizontal and vertical centre-lines faintly on top of the clay – as you did for the freehand face.

This time, of course, you need to build the face up in relief, according to the physical measurements you have taken. The highest point will be the tip of the nose and it is as well to identify this first. The height can be established by applying measurement A to E, which is item 14 on Fig. 39, and should be the same number on your list. Check this from both sides. The general position for the nose, you naturally relate to your centre-lines. You can mark in the hair line, C, at the correct distance from A, and identify – according to any of the other measurements taken – whatever additional features there may be for which you think it will be helpful to know their whereabouts at this stage. It would be unwise for me to give, or for you to work to, a rigid sequence. You want to work spontaneously, only taking time for measuring up when you consider it necessary before you can go forward.

An easy way to mark out essential points is with match heads or small indentations. You cannot mark all the measurements from the beginning; many can only be applied as

you proceed. For example, you cannot apply the eye measurements until after you have scooped out the eye sockets.
You may find that some marks get obliterated as you work –
and that match heads get buried. Don't worry. Just apply
the marks again. Remember to remove match heads when
their job is done or when you finish.

As before, do not fuss, for the moment, about achieving meticu-
lously exact dimensions, or trying to establish a final-looking face.
Everything can stay fairly 'rough' until you consider you
have a good overall shape of the right main dimensions.

You will now have to work closely to your model and
photographs. It is a good idea to develop the profile of the
face first. There are two important angles – shown in Fig. 40
– to establish: **a**, the brow angle and **b**, the chin angle.
(These 'angles' are relative to the vertical and to each other.)
Lay the side of a ruler lightly along the brow of the face, just
touching the tip of the nose (line **a**, Fig. 40). Study this
carefully and model the brow accordingly, just as it relates
to this straight line, noticing any irregularities and the dip
at the top of the nose.

Fig. 40. Face angles.

Now place the ruler on the tip of the nose and touching the chin. You want to relate angle (line) b to angle a, and/or a third angle, c, to a. (Both angles, b and c, may need a little manipulation of your ruler to get the best position, sometimes touching the nose, sometimes below.) The lips may intrude a little but these are the angles you must work to.

These 'face angles', or lines, help you to recognise the detail on the middle and lower part of the face to be taken into account; how far the nose protrudes, the contour of the lips, whether the chin recedes or protrudes and so on. Try to establish the correct relationship between the angles, b and c. The chin is not necessarily immediately below the brow. Also compare these angles and the detail with your measurements and your photographs.

You will find that your work will need constant refinement and changing. The more you can work with your live model the better. You have to keep focused towards your final objective; however, you will not achieve it at the first attempt. It is quite demanding, and, sometimes, quite frustrating and exhausting. If you pay attention to possible undercuts as you work, reducing them where you think they may become a problem, it will help considerably when casting this face in a one piece mould.

Work *directly from your model* fully to establish the final likeness. **Never guess the exact shape of features like the nostril bulbs, the lips or the eyes.** Study them individually and work on each one as accurately as you can. Sometimes I run a finger over a feature, such as an eye socket or the lips, to try to get a better feel for the shape. If you would like to see the surface as smooth as possible on the finished cast, you can, as one of your last steps, 'polish' the skin areas as explained from page 125. If there is hair to tidy up, define the edges quite clearly but leave the locks more by way of an impression than trying to suggest infinite detail. You might use a comb, sparingly, as for the earlier, freehand face in relief.

With these finishing touches all complete, do STOP!

Always warn your model not to expect a photographic likeness but, instead, hopefully at least, an exciting piece of sculpture. You are trying to be creative and creativity is not imitation. The purpose of it all is to create something and have fun, so do make sure your subject does not also expect some miracle. Most sculptors need quite a lot of experience before they can achieve a reasonably satisfactory result. This is just your beginning.

When Michelangelo was asked why a sculpture of Lorenzo de' Medici, which he had done in the Medici Chapel, looked 'nothing like him,' he replied, 'What does it matter? In a thousand years' time no one will know what he looked like anyway!'

If Michelangelo could do no better than this, what hope have you or I? Your objective is to enjoy the task, to learn from it and hopefully give pleasure to your model. I would encourage you to cast this head in relief which, if you have modelled it carefully, should be possible in a one piece mould. (Chapter 4 tells you how.) However, being fairly large and 'flat' it may break easily, so work very carefully. If you propose to mount or hang the finished work, don't forget to insert a piece of wood into the back of your cast before it sets (see page 95).

Chapter 9:

Modelling a Full Head

Before starting to model a full head in clay from life you will need photographs as suggested in the previous chapter, including, on this occasion, one of the back of the head and the neck. Try for an interesting and exciting pose.

Heads can be modelled, as I have done many times, without a support but I do not recommend the practice. (I mention this only because, if you cannot readily find a support, you might like to try. Should you do so, you must ensure that the head is firmly supported by the neck, which must reach right down to your work-board as in Fig. 41.) Furthermore, as the neck is narrower than the head, the unsupported structure will tend to be a little unstable. Although this has never caused me any special problems, I am always extra careful when casting or moving such a work. Having, however, a proper central support, securely fixed to a sufficiently large, wooden, base will give the head additional stability and should prevent it from ever getting knocked over.

Bust Peg

The basic support for a head is called a *bust peg* (see Fig. 42). This is a simple but larger version of the armature suggested for small standing figures in Chapter 6. It consists of a column made of suitable material and rigidly fixed at right angles into an appropriately-sized base. The

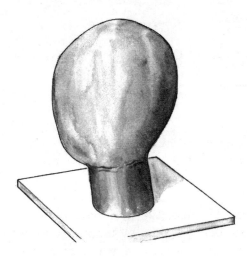

Fig. 41. Rough overall head shape.

most common material used for the peg is wood, about 1 to 1½ inches (2.5-3.75cm) square in section and of the height required to reach well up into the head. *You must fix the peg very securely* onto the base. There must be no looseness or movement between the two. This can be done with small, right-angle brackets screwed onto each side of the peg at its bottom end and then into the base, making sure all the screws are quite tight. In case you need to move your model whilst your work is in progress, it is handy to add two battens underneath the bust peg base – as in Fig. 42 – so that you can grasp it easily and safely from underneath. Ready-made bust pegs can be purchased and are very good but, unless you are going to do a lot of this work, they are perhaps not worth the additional expense.

On a bust peg the head will slip down if it is not supported from below by the neck. This can be overcome as explained below. However, for your first, full, three-dimensional head, *I strongly recommend that you arrange for*

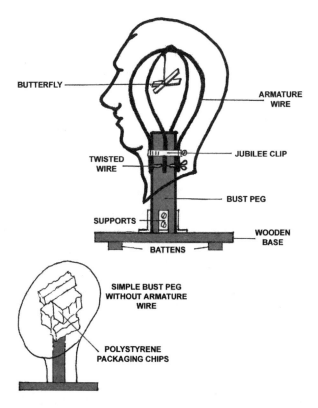

Fig. 42. Bust peg.

the neck of your subject to run down to rest firmly on the bust peg base. Then there will be no need to prevent the clay from slipping. The clay model of Marie, in Fig. 43, was modelled with her full neck like this. Having neck all the way down also makes matters much more simple if you want to cast your subject's head. Remember that, if you wish to keep the finished head in its clay model form, you may want to remove it from the bust peg. If so, the thing to do is to cover the peg with a thin plastic bag before you begin modelling. This tip was explained in more detail for the full torso in Chapter 7.

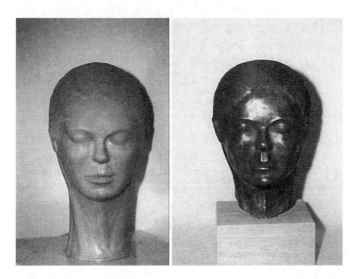

Fig. 43. Marie: clay model (left); cast (right).

Should you decide to attempt your full head without carrying the neck right down, then *you must arrange to prevent it slipping down the bust peg.* (Having done so you must accept that your bust peg cannot be removed.) There are three ways of doing this:

1. You can wrap some thick wire or cord round the bust peg in a spiralling manner but you must fix this securely so that it will not also slip with the clay. Small fencing 'staple' or 'pin' nails should hold it well.

2. Assuming your bust peg is wooden, you could knock in some nails where clay will cover them. These would rather resemble the branches of a tree. In addition, fix a simple, light *'butterfly'* (or wooden

cross) on top of the bust peg. (These are also used hanging – see 3 next.)

3.   The most professional way is to build a simple armature on the bust peg. This is shown in Fig. 42 and is made of two loops of metal, fixed securely and set at right angles to each other. Strips of metal or thick, stiff wire will do – but the best material is the aluminium armature wire sold by Tiranti's (see Appendix) and other suppliers. This is not expensive and it may be well worthwhile buying a small supply as it is also very useful for other work. Bend two suitable lengths of this wire into open-ended egg shapes about a couple of inches (5cm) smaller in diameter than your model's head – you need not be too fussy. At both ends of each one, form a 'leg' about 3 inches (7.5cm) long. Fix these legs in position as shown, tightly against your bust peg, using jubilee clips, staples or strong wire twisted together.

Economy with Clay

You can use clay alone for a full head and this is fine but, if you want to be economical with clay and keep your model's weight down, you can use other materials to pack out the centre of the head before you add the clay. Chunks of polystyrene packing material are excellent, as are bits of wood or chicken wire. Even old newspapers *screwed very tightly together* can be used – provided they are satisfactorily contained within a looped, armature area as suggested in method 3 above. (I once stuck a ball of garden string inside an armature like this – which proved perfectly adequate.)

      Old newspapers are NOT good enough for methods 1 or

2 where you have no armature. However, you can include other materials within the clay. See Fig. 42 inset. Make sure that they are held firmly together with blobs of clay.

If you choose, instead, to use solid clay, and have built an armature (method 3 above), it is advisable to hang a 'butterfly' in the centre. This can be seen in Fig. 42. (Butterflies, incidentally, are used quite often in sculpture, and are very useful when doing larger, standing figures.)

Into the Modelling

As always, think about the right clay for your purpose before you commence actual modelling. The choices have been outlined in earlier chapters but, to refresh your memory, glance back in particular to page 126. A head can look particularly fine in Potclays 1114 Craft Crank if you decide you are going to let it dry out to keep without casting any copies. An example is Laia in Fig. 46 which, incidentally, survived the casting process as well (Fig. 47).

Begin packing wads of clay together to start off your figure at the bottom of its neck. Build a strong column of clay of about the right width. See Fig. 39, item 6.

When you reach the level of the lower jaw, start enlarging it into a head shape. Provided your clay is packed really tightly together and not too damp, it should be self-supporting – including outside the circumference of the neck itself. Apply the clay in portions no bigger than golf balls, always working from the centre outward. Knock all the clay into position with a flat piece of wood or the edge of your fist. If you have packed the middle part of the head with other materials to save on clay, knock the clay you *are* using well into them.

When you have covered the bust peg with a large, homogenous mass of clay, you can start to consider the outside dimensions. Work towards the overall shape and size of your subject's head. You can see this stage in Fig. 41 – the lower front narrowing towards the chin and then back from the chin down to the neck with a smooth curve, the back of the head shaped smoothly inward to meet the neck below.

The usual way of applying clay at this stage is in little, round balls, each about the size of a small, glass marble. Flatten them a little with your thumb as you put them on but do not smooth them out too much; leave the 'potted' surface as much as you can.

Do not attempt any detail yet. Just keep the overall profile going, working towards your final figure without being too fussy.

It is a good idea, quite early, to mark out – faintly – your centre-lines as viewed from the front or back. As these are likely to get erased again whilst you work, the thing to do is also to sink a match at each extremity of these lines, so that you know both where they are and what their directions are, should you have to replace them. These matches then act as substitutes for the ends of the chalk or pencilled lines which were still visible on your work-board, and to which you worked, when you were doing the relief head. If your figure has hair, or a beard, you can begin to add clay in readiness for these.

When you are reasonably happy with the overall 'rough' shape and posture, you can start to work on the features. Again, do not be too concerned with accuracy at this stage. Just a simple overall impression is all you want. The more important consideration for the moment is that features are all in the right places. You have to keep on refining them all the time as you continue.

You can now establish the eye sockets on the eye line as before, remembering the relative dimensions. As with your measured relief head in the last chapter, it is worth establishing the nose next. Leave detail but check the distance **A** to **E** (Fig. 37) from both sides so that, spatially, the tip of the nose juts forward by the right amount. Then you can develop the angle of the forehead. Cut off surplus clay or add more where necessary. You need only to get this forehead profile about right, and carry it round the sides to the temples. Immediately underneath the forehead is the dip which you need to run smoothly inwards to meet the top of the nose and merge with the eye sockets either side. Model this carefully. You may need to adjust the upper nose shape, now that you have the forehead more developed and the dip in place. Work in a similar way for the chin by building up a little extra clay where necessary. (Check measurement A-B, Fig. 39, item 15.)

Establish these features and their proper relationships, as before, also by comparison, after laying a plastic ruler on your model. Do not develop the chin fully or start to model the lips. Remember, you are only concerned with the overall positions and angles for now.

Next it is probably time to develop further: (a) The jaw angles; that is, the angles at which the jaws define the lower edge at each side of the face and fall backwards from the mouth – and then gradually outwards towards the rear of the jaw bone, the *mandible*. Whilst there, you may want to build up the cheeks a little; (b) The arched curve below the chin to the neck; observe carefully so that you follow the contoured path this curve also exhibits as each side blends backward into the neck; (c) The general structure of the neck – in the female, especially, aim for a delicate slenderness and sweeping line; also suggest the sternocleidomastoid muscle (shown to good effect in my portrait of an African girl – in Fig. 44); (d) The hair as a single, well-shapen mass but without detail, adding more clay if needed.

You should, by now, have a figure which roughly resembles your subject's head but which remains still rather crude. That is fine. Now comes the exciting part as you begin refining the likeness to your model.

Fig. 44. African girl.
Head in clay supported by neck. First layer of plaster for two piece mould has been applied to the back of the head and the shims removed, ready for the second layer of plaster.

In general, follow the principles outlined for the measured head in relief of Chapter 8. This is a good moment to give your figure an all-round, thorough, dimensional check-up. You can cut away or add clay if you discover large inaccuracies but, normally, your next important step is the putting on of a few temporary markers at those points you are needing to measure to and from. For example, insert half-matchsticks with their heads just protruding at the cardinal points I introduced at Fig. 37.

Mark the measured width of your model's eyes, and the distance between them. I do not use matches for this but just make little indentations with the end of a pencil or modelling tool. If necessary, reinstate your very faint, vertical centre-lines to ensure your measurements are centralised and maintain a good balance. Mark out the line of the lips as in Fig. 39, item 5(a). Check that the lips end roughly in line with the pupil above on each side.

Confirm that the eye line is in the middle of the head as a whole – Fig. 34 will remind you.

Take a look at **B** to **F** (the fundamental depth of the full-size head oval from chin to top of cranium, item 18 in Fig. 39), **A** to **A** (item 1), **A** to **C** (item 13), **C** to **E** (item 12), **A** to **B** (item 15) and so on. However, *do not become too concerned about moderate inaccuracies.*

Whilst all the physical measurements you took were intended to be fairly precise, you have no need to stick too rigidly to them in the final result. It does not matter if you are a little out – it seems to add vigour to a figure that can escape if you stick too strictly to the measurements. I think it was Rodin who said, 'The more lifelike I try to make my figures, the more lifeless they seem to become.'

So, as you continue your modelling, let your work flow freely. From now on it is a matter of working freely, then checking; working and checking, as you go along.

From the positions of the nose and eyes you should be able to establish those of the ears. Behind point **A** on both sides, and at a suitable distance back, place a D-shaped slab of clay roughly the size of the respective ears. Take and use any additional measurements that you feel might be helpful at any time. This may be difficult if your subject is not present but you can establish approximations from photographs. I will return to the ears presently.

Check the highest point of the cranium, **F**. If it is too high – or low – adjust as appropriate and re-check the **B**-**F** measurement. Once you have it right, carefully re-model the contours of the head back towards point **F** again. (Note that **F** is, in reality, below the hair. You may therefore need to remove some 'hair' and then restore it again afterwards.)

In more detail

Work away at all the features, gradually refining as you proceed. Keep the whole face in balance all the time. Try not to concentrate too much on one part whilst neglecting the rest. It is important that all parts continue to relate to each other, once each has been established. As with the measured face in relief in Chapter 8, **never guess shapes or contours, such as around the eyes, ears, nose or chin. Study your model, or photographs, fully and attentively.** Continue to look and, when you look, search for information carefully. Keep checking as you go along.

Most of the features of the face are fairly straightforward and I covered them in the last chapter. However, the eyes, ears and hair can present a few more traps:

Eyes. If you study sculptures of the past, you will soon realise that the eyes seem to have been a problem for even the greatest sculptors. The basic problem I stated in my Introduction: you cannot carve the colour of the eyes. There is also another feature of the eyes which you cannot carve; and that is moisture. It is the colour combined with the moisture which gives vitality and 'life' to the eyes.

Throughout the centuries sculptors have tried many different methods of bringing 'life' to the eyes. Some have made holes, some partial holes; some have tried to carve the iris. A friend of mine marks the centre of the eyes with the head of a six-inch nail! I am not enamoured by any method I have seen. One drawback is that, if you attempt to carve holes or identify the irises, it is difficult to make them appear to be looking in the same direction.

In the end I come back to basics. I consider only the basic shape of the eye, the 'orange segment' referred to before (Chapter 8), and leave it at that, without trying to identify the pupil or the iris. Many Greek sculptures are like this. However, you are still left with the problem of the eyelids, which are quite difficult. Model these as explained in Chapter 8 for modelling a freehand face in relief.

When I did the head of my granddaughter Marie in Fig. 43, I decided, as an experiment, to model her with closed eyes. I thought this would give a lovely overall shape. To my surprise, it worked very well. Curiously enough, it did not appear that the eyes were closed; nobody noticed or mentioned it. Since then I have seen a head of another girl with her eyelids shut, and I thought she also had most beautifully shaped eyes.

So, I recommend keeping the eyes as simple as possible, concentrating mainly on the overall shape. You must experiment to find a solution to your satisfaction. Do remember, you cannot achieve the impossible.

Ears. I often wish ears hadn't been invented! I cannot find anything lovely about the ears but they are there and, if necessary, you must give them full attention if your figure is to be convincing. I say, 'if necessary', because quite often they are covered with hair. (See Laia in Fig. 46.) The ear is a very complex structure deserving specific study on your live model. Ears differ quite considerably and can look rather ugly if not modelled with care. It is as well to take the outside measurements on each one using your callipers. Work carefully from these on the two D-shaped slabs of clay you have already attached.

From your experience so far, you will realise that ears are rather vulnerable to drying out, getting damaged or broken off. Fill in behind the ears as much as you can, and flatten them towards the scalp a little. (I think it is justified to 'flatter' your subject a little – as I often do!) In the process make sure you leave just a thin, peripheral, outer lip, the *helix*, to each ear, to make them convincing. The helix surrounds an inner ridge of cartilage. Just suggest this, and ensure it runs smoothly into the helix without an undercut. Below that are the inner folds of the ear. Do not make these

Fig. 45. Ear of David by Michelangelo.

too deep, or you will have great difficulty in casting. Just suggest the shape and leave them as shallow and smooth as you can. Fig. 45 is a photograph of Michelangelo's ear of David. The helix looks rather thick and heavy. This, probably, is because Michelangelo – working in marble – was afraid it might easily get broken off. However, perhaps one should also take into account the sheer scale of this huge work.

Hair. So far in this chapter, apart from getting its mass in place and shaped-up, the hair has been rather neglected. In order to capture a suitable look, you can cover the surface with small pellets of clay and leave it at that – a 'granulated' appearance often turns out surprisingly well – or you can refine the hair with a comb or perhaps even a dining fork. I once used a wire brush! You must experiment. You may well not achieve the desired effect first time. Often, I have to make several attempts with different 'tools' before I achieve an acceptable result. Remember, this is one of the advantages of clay; it is so malleable that, provided you keep it moist, you can go on revising, altering and changing for

Fig. 46. Laia in clay.

quite some time. (It is worthwhile drawing your attention to a head I recently saw modelled by a young student. She was determined to apply the hair in 'strands' – to look realistic. Unfortunately, most of it fell off as it dried out, and the rest came off in the mould. Hair **must** be applied in good solid masses.)

Notice the figure on the cover of this book by **Tom Gordon**. This is a splendid example of modelling at its best. Tom has applied the hair in one large mass, hidden the ears and carried the hair on down to support the head. Just as it should do, the model displays the characteristic of looking quite 'finished' even though more work could be done. See Chapter 7, page 124.

Finishing Off

As I have warned repeatedly, the difficulty is knowing when to stop. If you are not careful you can go on refining and refining until your figure loses its vitality.

Making a Mould and Casting

If you intend to cast the head, it is best done vertically with a two piece mould. Select your separation line carefully. I usually run this line just behind the helix of the ears, but where you position it depends upon the features of your model. If you have remembered to build up a little clay behind the ears you should avoid any undercut problems there; have a last glance round for any other potential undercuts which might be averted.

Fig. 47. Laia cast.

Chapter 4 takes you through the entire process, so refer back there, when you need to. If you do not want to include the whole length of the neck, you can make a wall around it at the level where you want to stop. For interest this can be done at an angle as in Figs. 43, the cast, and 47.

Colouring

Colour, patination or other finishes can all be used on cast, sculptured heads. The techniques can all be found at the end of Chapter 4.

Mounting a Head

Whilst I dealt briefly with mounting also at the end of Chapter 4, it is quite difficult to mount a full head in plaster and I DO NOT recommend it for the beginner.

(If you have modelled the head without a bust peg, or, perhaps, using one which will slip out, and only intend keeping your figure in clay rather than making a sturdier copy, this should continue to stand happily on the base of its neck. If the head is on a permanent bust peg, being one which extends well below the figure itself, and, likewise, your wish is to leave it to dry for keeping and display, you can sometimes, with great care, subsequently attach this bust peg to a better mount. However, it is definitely a tricky operation and you may need help.)

Normally, having made a mould, if you are then most careful in the casting to keep level what will become the base of the neck, you can display your figure without any separate mount. You shouldn't run into any problems with the cast standing solidly that can't be alleviated by a little judicious sanding once the plaster is absolutely dry. To prevent this base causing harm to furniture or paintwork, see Chapter 4, page 85.

Another idea, which I find interesting and simple, is to cast only the front, or face, of the head. This is not the same thing as a relief figure but is, in effect, a 'mask'. You can make it as deep as you like and stop the (vertical) half-mould wherever you like. Do this by letting the moulding plaster run freely down the sides of the face or by means of using a clay 'partition'. Figs. 48(a) and 48(b)

Fig. 48(a). Mask.

show an example which I cast, in plaster, from a full-size head. I did not build a clay wall but, in this instance, let the plaster run freely – which gave the figure a nice rugged edge. It was quite easy to remove the mould and fill it with plaster for the cast. You will notice I inserted a piece of wood in the back of the cast so that I could screw on the mounting post.

On this occasion, I used for the mounting post a small, square, table leg, with a flange, bought in a DIY shop in Portugal. I drilled two holes horizontally through the post (or leg) so that I could insert screws into the wood block in the back of the cast to hold the mask firmly. I finished this plaster cast face to resemble bronze. (The original full head in clay was a commission, already cast in bronze, and which stood on the neck without a mount.)

Fig. 48(b). Mask mounting.

Chapter 10:

Constructions

It is generally considered that sculpture is created either by modelling in a malleable material or by carving from a solid substance. Constructions do not fall into either category but, nevertheless, are considered to be sculptures because they are, essentially, three-dimensional. The idea of assembling various materials to make a sculpture goes back to the beginning of the twentieth century but it did not capture the imagination of many artists or the public.

However, in the last few decades, it seems to have had a growing popularity. There are, probably, several reasons for this. First there was the imaginative work of Pablo Picasso. Previously, the 'Constructivists' were mainly Russian artists who were little known but Picasso could not be ignored. Then there were the 'mobiles' of the American sculptor, Alexander Calder. An example is represented by Fig. 49. These were novel, fascinating, fun and available; you could find room for them in or around the house. Together, they gave a respectability to constructional art and were enthused over by the new post World War II population. Furthermore, construction art appealed to those who wanted to be creative but did not want to go through years of conventional training. It appeared to be easy to execute, achieve a result and provide great fun. Although, needless to say perhaps, all the great constructivists, including Picasso, had been well trained in the conventional disciplines.

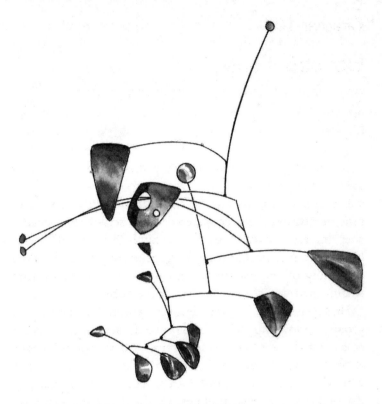

Fig. 49. Drawing from Alexander Calder mobile.

Materials

The introduction of new materials and adhesives in recent years opened up vast new fields in this area. Perspex, resins, PVA (polyvinyl acetate), polystyrene, epoxies and cyanoacrylates (for example, superglue) have all created new and exciting possibilities.

It could be said that any material may be used for constructions. A friend of mine who did most exciting work used to search rubbish tips. What you will not find is the imagination. That must be your contribution and it must come from within. There is no limit to the materials you can use but you may find limitations arise from the methods needed to hold them together.

Metals, generally, need welding or brazing for rigid construction. However, small metal constructions can be held together with wire, some modern adhesives or both used together. Bind the join with several strands of interlocking, flexible wire (copper wire is the best), then paint the join with an adhesive. Superglue only works under slight pressure and so has to be used cautiously but Araldite or a similar epoxy resin would be satisfactory. (These glues are generally rather thick and do not run in easily but leave a nice smooth finish.) Sheet metals can be joined with epoxy resins but you may have to hold them rigidly together until set. Cyanoacrylate (superglue) is a very remarkable and useful adhesive but, like all things, has its limitations. Always remember that the way a work – any work – is constructed is important to the final strength and stability of the work. Two pieces of metal joined together at right angles, for example, would probably soon come apart but, if you made a box, that would hold together better because of the support from the other sides.

Superglue is excellent for ceramics and sets very quickly. However, it only sets under *slight* pressure. This makes it so curious. Apply no pressure at all and it will not set but neither will it set if you put on too much pressure.

Wood is excellent for constructions, and ordinary, PVA (polyvinyl acetate) white, wood glue is quite suitable. The work has to be held until set; this can be done with clamps, binding or pin nails.

Cardboard, cartridge and corrugated paper are all suitable materials. There is also available a white, double-sided card with polystyrene sandwiched in between. This is an excellent material and can be used to great effect. It comes in various thicknesses, is rigid and can be easily cut with a

Stanley knife. Fig. 52 (top) was made with this. MDF (medium-density fibreboard) is another material which is excellent. Stronger and in larger sizes than polystyrene board it comes in various thicknesses. The thinner sizes can be cut with a Stanley knife. Available from builders' merchants, wood yards and DIY stores. Use wood glue.

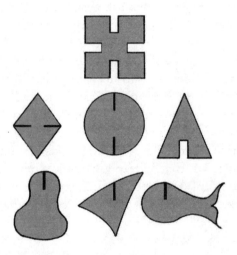

Fig. 50. Interlocking shapes.

A very useful way of joining flat surfaces at right angles is by means of interlocking joints. Some shapes with these are given in Fig. 50. The advantage of these joints is that they can be changed around to make different constructions but, if you want them to remain fixed, a small amount of glue may be inserted between them at the join. Make these in almost any flat material, for example, wood, cardboard, metal, polystyrene board or MDF. The slot needs to be the same thickness as the material. If you make several of the same shape, you can build them up into various interesting constructions or they can be used for mobiles.

Expanded polystyrene is a very interesting and useful product. Use the blocks of it you find in television and other packing boxes. This material can be cut quite easily with a hot wire. Special 'hot wire' cutters can be bought quite cheaply at art and craft shops. Be careful with adhesives; make sure they are suitable for expanded polystyrene as some simply dissolve it. This material is great fun and stretches the imagination. It is impossible to work in fine detail. Therefore you are compelled to work in large masses – which I consider provides very good experience.

Another interesting material is papier mâché. All manner of quite wonderful figures can be created with this material. Old newspapers are quite good for this, and there is no need to tear them up and soak them, as people did in the past. Just tear the sheets into smaller pieces and put layer upon layer, pasting each layer with inexpensive wallpaper glue. For most work you will need a 'former' upon which to lay the paper. A 'former' is any form or shape upon which you can lay and build up the paper. You can use any common object, such as a vase, a doll's face, even the back of your hand. Alternatively, you can make your own unusual shapes. These can be made with Plasticine or constructed from old bits of wood, chicken wire or expanded polystyrene. The finished article can be effectively painted with poster or powder paints and covered with a fixative.

I have seen some very fine work made with the lovely, semi-transparent, Japanese papers which are available from good art shops. A very fine, translucent, bowl can be made by laying this paper over an upside-down pudding basin – the 'former'. Do not trim the edges. Leave them 'unfinished' like petal edges. Don't use too many layers. No further colouring is required but delicate flower petals or leaves can be inserted between the layers of paper during the making, if you wish. These are quite lovely.

Yet another idea is to make a rough, abstract shape out of

scrap materials and drape a rag, soaked in plaster of Paris, over it. When this sets, you will have an interesting rigid figure. Use your imagination to create exciting shapes.

You will have to make your own decisions about how best to join various materials together. I hope that my remarks thus far in this chapter will help. However, you can always experiment. Only the other day I joined two round pieces of polished metal together with superglue. Quite honestly, I did not expect this to work. I left them joined together overnight and, since then, I have been quite unable to pull them apart. The lesson to learn from this is that you must leave most adhesives plenty of time to set fully and 'cure'. (I once repaired a valuable, 4,000-year-old Mayan vase, which had been smashed to pieces, by reconstructing it in this way using only Superglue.)

There is no limit to what can be done with old materials – one friend of mine used old piano pieces with great aesthetic effect. Nuts, bolts, screws, washers, bits of old clocks, bicycles, prams and almost any other discarded metals and materials can all be used imaginatively. There is one lady sculptor who even makes remarkable large figures from broken glass bottles. She first makes a steel framework – armature – and then attaches the pieces of broken glass with wire.

I have seen remarkable work produced from discarded tin cans. In Kenya, I once bought an oil lamp made from one, and used for lighting mud huts. The ingenuity and skill were remarkable. In Portugal an old fellow makes wonderful models of ships from them. Some readers may have seen the tin toys made in Germany after the First World War. Inside the toy can be seen the colourful stamp of the original container. These toys are now collectors' items and fetch very high prices. A talented friend of mine makes wonderful human figures cut from old cans. The tin is cut to resemble a muscle, shawl, skirt or some other dynamic feature and then these pieces are soldered together.

With a tin can, cut off both ends with the type of tin opener which removes the entire end including the lip. Then, with tin snips, cut down the length of the cylinder, along the seam, and open it out. With a little beating, you will now have a nice piece of tinplate. (Take care not to cut or damage your fingers. Except when I am working in clay, I wear protective gloves most of the time. It is surprising how often you can nick your skin.)

You can do much the same with large metal tubes like those in which tomato purée is sold. Cut off the bottom – strong scissors that have long since lost their sharpness will do this if you have no tin snips – and then cut down the length of the tube and remove the top. After rinsing, you will have a useful piece of metal which is very malleable and so soft that it can be incised with a blunt tool to great effect. You can make very interesting sketches and designs in this material. Open out the piece you are working with and rest it on a thick pad of cloth. Then press the design into it with a blunt pencil or modelling tool. One friend of mine makes her own Christmas cards this way, sticking the metal design onto cardboard.

Design

Generally, I prefer abstract designs for construction work but there are exceptions. Perhaps we should first consider what we mean by 'abstract'. Different artists seem to apply different meanings. For some it means abstracting the essence of the subject or reducing it to a minimum – 'minimalism' as some call it. For me 'abstract' means 'like no other known thing'. The subject represents nothing but itself and cannot be identified as anything else. It is extremely difficult to design something which is genuinely abstract. In reality perhaps we can only really think about what we know, and this is not abstract. I have spent many hours puzzling over this problem and trying to make abstract designs. Several examples I have made are included in this chapter. Both Figs. 51 and 52 were first made in polystyrene sandwich board and, later, re-worked as permanent pieces in metal from a scrapyard. Fig. 51, Wings, was finally cut from an old copper hotwater cylinder. Apart from an abstract design –'like nothing else' – I wanted to carry light along the threads joining the sides, so I used heavy nylon fishing line. (Glass optic-fibre would have been more effective, I have since learned!) I also wanted to make a contrast between the metals and the base. I was lucky enough to find, on the seashore in Portugal, a lovely piece of black stone, containing scattered streaks of copper-coloured mineral which reflected the copper wings. Other than drilling a hole in the stone for the central column, I did no work on the stone base at all.

You could easily make this figure using the polystyrene white board for the wings. Carefully pierce small holes all round the edge of each circular wing, equidistant apart, and then make a larger hole in each one to receive the cross bar. The upright and cross bar can be made of wooden dowel sticks with a simple overlap joint glued together. Using the white board, I suggest you find a single length of thick black thread for the crossing strands. Paint the central support to suit your taste – a dark blue or an autumnal colour would look well. You must do this before you start the threading. This is quite a tricky job. The whole assembly should be threaded with a single thread but the cross strands have to be lined up diagonally. You also have to ensure that the cross strands do not collide with the crossbar – so the original placing of this is quite critical. It is best to try things out, with a test run, before you start. The cross strands must also be tight enough not to sag but not too tight or they will distort the wings. Fortunately, with board

Fig. 51. Wings.

and thread, you can fix each strand where it passes through an edge of wing hole with a dab of glue – which was not possible for me with nylon and metal. A mahogany or a black stand will enhance your figure.

The title of Fig. 52, Hollow Bowl, may intrigue you. This work was not intended to be a figure at all. At the time I wanted to carve an oval bowl with very precise contours from marble. So, from white polystyrene board, and as if looking down, in plan, from above, I cut an oval shape having both the external dimension and also the internal shape which I wanted. This was effectively a template for the top edge of the bowl. In addition, I cut out two semi-ovals, the internal contours of which matched the external dimensions of the bowl lengthways and crossways. I then carved the marble bowl to match these shapes. These 'profiles' lay around for months as I had no further use for them.

Fig. 52. Hollow bowl.

However, after some time, it occurred to me that they would make an attractive construction if assembled together as in Fig. 52 (top). This was so admired by friends that I decided to make, in heavy copper, the replica in Fig. 52 (bottom). I think this 'genesis' is interesting because it demonstrates how important it is constantly to be aware of interesting shapes.

The spiral figure in Fig. 53(a) and (b) proved more difficult to create than I first thought. If you want an interesting design problem try to draw an accurate spiral on a flat surface, with spacing that widens as you proceed outwards from the centre and then narrows towards the end. However, to save you the trouble, I have drawn Fig. 54. This can be enlarged on most photocopiers. Good quality picture-mount board would be suitable for making this abstract construction.

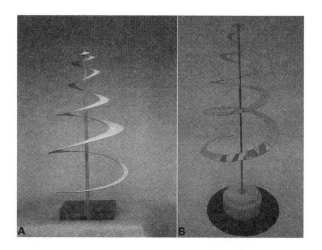

Fig. 53. Spiral.

Fig. 54. Spiral on flat surface.

You need to trace your enlarged spiral so that you can transfer the drawing on to your mount board. Then make a small hole in the centre and cut out the spiral. Mount a dowel stick with a pointed top in a wooden base, and then suspend the spiral from it, stretching it out a little. My final figure here was made in copper. My original objective was for a larger outdoor figure which would revolve and shimmer in the sunlight. However, it took me a long time to work out the spiral, and the result, so far, was made the same size but in copper. This, seen in Fig. 53(b), was quite pleasing.

The constructions shown in Fig. 55 are based on the Golden Section or Mean, a fascinating, mathematical ratio of approximately 5:8, attributed to Euclid and used in the design of the Parthenon. It is considered to be quite beautiful and has been used in art and architecture ever since. Even Van Gogh used this proportion in some of his portraits.

You begin your model by drawing a line; then dividing that line into two unequal parts so that the ratio of the two parts is 5:8. Upon this line you can construct a rectangle, the sides of which will have the same ratio. This has been done in Fig. 56 with rectangle **ADHC**.

My trial construction (shown in Fig. 55, top and middle pictures) was first made of corrugated paper and proved to be intriguing to observers. I stood this on stiff mount board of, roughly, 18 x 14 inches (45 x 35cm) but this size is not critical. Central to your mount board draw the largest rectangle (**ADHC**) taken from Fig. 56. Mine was 11½ x 7¼ inches (29 x 18cm). Although the Golden ratio is, in fact, an approximation based on mathematical theory, your drawings will have to be as precise as possible. Some minor discrepancies are bound to creep in but you can ignore these.

Divide the base line of the rectangle into two unequal

Fig. 55. Golden Mean figure.

segments with the ratio between them of 5:8. On mine these were approximately 7¼ inches (18cm) and 4¼ inches (11cm). Then divide the rectangle up into two squares and a smaller rectangle as shown. (For the convenience of construction I placed the larger square (**ADEB**) on the left – but you can suit yourself about this.) The larger square has, of course, 7¼ (18cm) sides; the smaller one (**BFGC**) having 4¼ inch (11cm) sides. The space above the smaller square will be a rectangle of the same proportions as the original rectangle which can, again, be divided up similarly (theoretically, you could go on dividing indefinitely!).

In both squares, draw a curve – using a pair of compasses, each time centred at the opposite corner of the square by which it is contained. You should now have a graceful, diminishing, joined up curve identical to that shown by **D-B-G** in Fig. 56. My sculpture was based upon this curve as extended into the smaller rectangle (**FEHG**) and so on. (Do not try to continue the internal curve too far as it would be impossible to construct the final model too small anyway.) Determine the total length of your curve when your drawing work is complete, by placing a piece of garden wire – or string – over it. Cut out a rectangular sheet of corrugated paper of this length. I suggest you make the width of this sheet just under half its length. (This width measurement defines the height of your finished construction (see Fig. 55) to the top of the inside apex. The corrugated sheet for my figure was 16 inches (40cm) long by 7¼ inches (18cm) wide.)

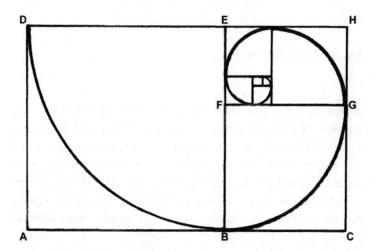

Fig. 56. Golden Mean diagram.

Cut this sheet diagonally in half. Gently roll one of the resultant right-angle triangles, corrugated side out, and locate it carefully on your mount board, following the curve you have drawn. Apply a little adhesive to the bottom of the triangle, or to the board, and carefully attach the triangle, starting from the centre. UHU or white PVA (polyvinyl acetate) wood glue will be quite satisfactory. I had to use panel pins to hold mine in position until it set. (Ordinary sewing pins were not strong enough.) I first drove these through the mount board to locate the relevant position of the holes along the curve; then inverted the board and drove them back through the same holes to hold the figure in position until the PVA glue set. The figure was quite rigid when the glue set and I was able to remove the panel pins from below. (These were all tricky little operations which required a measure of experimentation!)

You can paint or spray your figure with acrylics or emulsion. Car or domestic paint sprays are not suitable. I rather liked the rough texture and colour of the corrugated paper so I left mine as it is. Subsequently, I made the same figure using wooden dowelling as shown in the bottom picture of Fig. 55. The underlying idea was for a much larger, outdoor, work using hefty posts like telegraph poles. Not only do I think this would be an awesome outdoor sculpture but it could also be great fun for children to run around and play in. (Note: You do not have to stick to my size for this construction. I made one model half this size and another twice as big but the calculations do get more difficult. I had to use a calculator – which often took me to several decimal places!)

Mobiles – such as the one shown in Fig. 49 – are fascinating and not difficult to make with a little imagination. They can be made of almost any material. The component parts can be connected with thread and glue. The interlocking joints, described earlier in this chapter, can also be used to great effect. Mobiles can be displayed free standing on a suitable support, or hung from a ceiling. You have to be careful where you position your suspension points so that the weight will balance in the way you want. Cheap coat-hangers you get from dry cleaners can be very useful. The wire bends and cuts easily. A good tip when you tie threads to wire is to secure the knot with a dab of universal glue.

The ideas I have given here are just a few to get you started. Now you are on your own. Let your imagination run free and I am sure you will find this branch of sculpture both interesting and very exciting.

Chapter 11:

Carving

I said in the Introduction that I considered modelling and carving as branches of the same subject: sculpture. Some sculptors confine their whole interest to either one or the other; others work on both. So far in this book, with the exception of the last chapter, on Constructions, I have concentrated on modelling for the reasons I gave earlier: the material is cheap; it requires hardly any special tools to work with; and you can do so almost anywhere.

Carving is very different. Mostly, the materials are quite expensive. If you use wood, you have to ensure that it is of good quality – although, with luck, pieces can sometimes be found lying around. The tools must also be of good quality and they can be quite expensive. Ordinary carpenters' chisels and hammers will not be satisfactory.

Above all, you need some space, preferably set aside. Even with wood, chippings and sawdust fly all over the place. With stone, carving can be quite hazardous. I recommend protective clothing for all carving – including a dust mask, hair cap, goggles, gloves and overalls. As far as I am concerned this is all worthwhile and, whilst I have probably spent more than the average sculptor on equipment, it still represents less outlay over the longer term than many people spend on hobbies like golf or sailing. (I might add that along the way I have treated myself to a few 'luxury' items which are not essential.)

Nonetheless, I want properly to introduce you to carving,

not only to complete your considerations but in the hope that at least some of you may 'get the bug'. Rewarding as modelling can be, there is nothing like carving. It is the ultimate challenge.

As throughout the book, I recommend working as inexpensively as is possible. You should manage to keep your costs quite low whilst the space required can remain reasonably minimal, as before.

Your previous work and experience will stand you in good stead when carving and you will achieve some very good results.

I have divided this brief introduction to carving into four parts:

General principles, tools and equipment

Simple exercise piece

More advanced carving

Working a figure from life.

General Principles, Tools and Equipment

The number of different materials that can be carved is quite surprising. I suppose any material which has a depth can be carved, although some may be much more difficult to work than others. Most people will be aquainted with whittling, an ancient craft usually confined to embellishing walking sticks. All you need for this is a good sharp penknife and a nice, straight branch from a tree. Those who specialise in this craft take it a lot further and collect special knives and timbers.

The very first carving I made, a simple figure, was from a tablet of soap using an ordinary penknife. (They were all I had available at the time.) Soap is quite useful to practise on but, unfortunately, has a strong smell. Special waxes can be bought for modelling and carving which are used often by professionals. You can even carve a nice large potato, which is great fun. An advantage of potato is that you are forced to employ large and dramatic shapes. Expanded polystyrene can be carved very effectively. However, this needs a special, heated wire cutter which you can buy from art and craft shops. Odd bits of wood or fine blocks of it can all be carved using chisels, knives and rasps.

However in this book I am only going to consider direct carving in plaster. This might surprise some who consider wood or stone more desirable, but I am using plaster for the same reasons given in the first paragraph of this chapter.

Nevertheless, highly successful and dramatic results can also be achieved working in plaster. It was used considerably by Henry Moore, for example, for some of his largest works.

Fig. 57. Plaster block in casting box.

First of all, you need a block of pre-set plaster to carve. The size and shape of your block is not important; that may depend upon what kind of receptacle you have available to cast it in but, the larger the better. Use the same plaster mainly used for casting as before. (Mix 2; see Chapter 4.) I usually set my plaster blocks in plastic boxes, as they make it so easy to cast and to remove. Rectangular boxes of various sizes are, generally, the most useful. If the box is plastic there is no need to treat it with a special release agent; a very thin wipe over with cooking oil will suffice. Pour the plaster mix into your box and shake or bang it about a little to help release any trapped air. When set quite cold the block should come out, with a little gentle persuasion, quite easily. If necessary, let a little air in at the sides to break the suction. Should you need some different shape or an extra large block, you may need to make up a special box for casting it. (White-faced chipboard is a good material for this job.) It may then be more difficult to remove your cast block than from a plastic box. Therefore, I make mine so that they can be dismantled easily, as in Fig. 57. With such a box, treat the inside with a suitable release agent (for which see Chapter 4, page 52), and push some clay into the joints before you pour in wet plaster.

A plastic box is hardly likely to be absolutely square, especially at the ends. This is of no consequence except that the surface which will become the base upon which your figure will stand, usually an end, must be square. If it is not, correct the problem before you get started with the carving. Stand the block, that end down, on a flat surface of medium sandpaper; rub well, and rotate as you go, until that bottom end has become trued-up. Check for uprightness with a simple set square.

Reliefs can also be carved in plaster. My one shown in Fig. 58 was carved in plaster, using only a simple wood chisel. (I cast the plaster block for this in a shallow oven tray.) This was a study for a much larger work to be executed in marble.

Tools

To start with, the fewer and simpler tools you have the better. The basic tool is the chisel but for cast plaster you do

Fig. 58. Family plaque.

not need special sculptors' chisels. Old wood chisels are excellent – I use them all the time for this work – and they do not want to be too sharp. All you need is a nice edge without it being razor sharp. If you can find two or three in small sizes, so much the better.

Next, a small mallet would be useful. The sort you used to get in boys' woodwork sets would be excellent. After starting this book I tried a cheap, meat tenderising mallet. I had never used one before but it seemed to be suitable. I removed the points with a saw, and shortened the handle by about 2 inches (5cm) as in Fig. 59. It turned out to be surprisingly useful! You do not want a heavy or large mallet. If you cannot find a small mallet, a lightweight hammer will do; however, the mallet is better because it has a larger, more balanced head and distributes the weight more evenly. Three inexpensive rasps will be useful: one coarse, one medium (but not fine) and a half round rasp cover most needs. 'Abrafiles' are also excellent for removing plaster. Rummage around markets, car-boot sales and junk shops. A small, sharp-pointed, paring knife or penknife will come in handy. You may like to have a couple of sheets of fine sandpaper for finishing; however, I have never found anything as satisfactory as the chisel for this purpose. A fine 'whisker', removed from plaster with a chisel, will leave a crisp, clean, sharp surface. I often use the edges and corners of the chisel, held on its side, for getting into difficult areas. I used no other tool on the relief shown in Fig. 58 – and there is some pretty fine detail on it.

Fig. 59. Mallet.

A small saw is useful. The best buy is a coping saw. These are not expensive at DIY stores. You can buy special round blades for them, which cut in all directions without having to turn the saw round, and they are very handy for this type of work. You must experiment a little with tools to find ones which will serve your purpose. A nail file, a broken hacksaw blade, odd knives, screwdrivers and the sandpaper files used for manicure are all useful.

Holding Work

The problem of holding your carving whilst you work is important. Overall, vices are not very useful for plaster work unless your carving is to have two, parallel flat surfaces and, even then, these surfaces can easily be damaged.

Never hold the work in one hand whilst you try to carve with the other hand. This applies especially when working with chisels – which brings me to a Golden Rule of craftsmanship:

WHEN WORKING WITH SHARP TOOLS ALWAYS ENSURE THAT BOTH YOUR HANDS ARE BEHIND – AND PROTECTED FROM – THE CUTTING EDGE OF THE TOOL.

Apply the rule no matter what material or tool you are using. This may sound obvious but you would be surprised to know how many cut hands I have seen – even amongst experienced sculptors.

There are three satisfactory ways of holding the work:

1. *A retaining board.* This is like the work-board you used for clay but you fix, rigidly, two battens of wood at a right angle to each other on the top. These battens will then prevent the work from sliding forward or slipping sideways as you work. The retaining board itself, of course, needs to be prevented from moving. I stand mine on a piece of material sold for preventing carpets from slipping but a non-slip bath safety mat may be equally suitable.

2. *A bag of sand.* The bag needs to be made of a fairly strong, cloth fabric. (Plastic bags only split open.) Hessian sacking is not much good for indoor work, because the sand tends to run out but I do use it outdoors. A handy size is about 18 x 10 inches (45 x 25cm). Fill this no more than two-thirds full with dry, ordinary, washed, builders' sand. The open end of your bag needs to be tightly sewn up. Place your carving on the bag and you will find that the sand within the bag can then be pushed around for support.

3. *A sand tray.* Similar in use to the sand bag, you need a tray of sand having strong sides. A deep oven tray will

do, or you could make a tray with sides about 2 inches (5cm) deep. (Were they to be any deeper they would interfere with your arms when working.) The sand wants to be filled to about half an inch (1.25cm) below the top. Nestle your block of plaster on the sand and work away. Always keep your sand dry.

Carving in plaster is not really dirty work as the material removed cleans up easily and does not leave stains. You will have a fair amount of plaster dust and chippings but if you spread some old newspapers around, you can easily enough collect all the debris together.

Holding your Chisel

Although cast plaster when set is quite soft and cuts easily, a firm grip on your chisel is essential. There will be times when you want to use the chisel alone, without a mallet; for example, when paring away small amounts of plaster. For right-handed people, grasp the centre of the chisel handle firmly by the right hand. (When I was a small boy I was taught to place my index finger along the blade of a saw when using it. Good professionals always do this as it gives the saw a sense of direction and rigidity. I do not know whether doing the same thing is common practice with carvers but, for me, it has become such a life-long habit that I invariably do so when using chisels. Certainly, it seems to be very effective.) Now place your left hand over the right, including that index finger. When working with hands and chisel alone, remember that two hands are *always* much better than one. Should you be left-handed, swap over these two hand positions.

Using your Chisel with a Mallet

I must here emphasise the need for practice. There will be times when, for more delicate work, using your chisel with a mallet is to be preferred. The chisel may otherwise shoot forward and take off more than you want. The same applies to all materials. This can be disastrous. With a mallet, you will only take off as much as a gentle tap cuts. As a right-hander, I hold my chisel firmly in my left hand and use my right hand for the mallet. Carving plaster in this way is a very delicate but satisfactory operation, and I quite enjoy the gentle, controlled tapping needed to achieve my purpose.

Simple Practice

It is a good idea to get a little practice before starting to carve a figure. Take a block of plaster and, with the chisel held almost parallel to the longer direction of the block, gently, without using a mallet, pare off the corner between two surfaces. Take off the thinnest paring you can. Then continue paring away until you have made a nice bevel of about 45°. Do not attempt to take off the whole bevel in one cut. It is best to mark this out before you start and then work down to the marks. (For 45°, your marks must be equidistant from the edge on both surfaces.)

This kind of controlled work is essential to good carving. When you have cut one bevel, make another on one end, at right angles to the first. Round off the corner between them, as you go, so that you will have a smooth curve joining both bevels. I enjoy doing this kind of exercise, each time aiming at perfection. It is rather like doing the finger exercises that most musicians practise regularly.

Simple Exercise Piece

For your first model I suggest the abstract figure shown in Fig. 60. I designed this for this book so as to embody the above techniques and produce an interesting finished article.

Fig. 60. Abstract.

First, cast a quite large, rectangular, block of plaster. For my example, I made the box shown in Fig. 57 from MDF, 10 x 3 x 3 inches (25 x 8 x 8cm), held together with pin nails so that it could be easily broken apart to release the block.

The aim of this exercise – using only a flat, wood chisel – is to create two flat surfaces, each carved into opposite sides of the block and having both convex and concave, curved ends. The wider the chisel, the better; a one inch (25mm) size would be perfect.

Begin with marking out the work with a pencil. Choose a top side for your block and draw a centre-line along this. Continue the line down across the centre of both ends. Now decide how deep you would like the first, cut-out surface to be and, at this depth from the top side, draw a straight and level line along one edge of the block. I suggest a depth of *just less than half* the thickness of the block. This choice will simplify matters when you come to the second half. Now, following Fig. 61, mark out the two opposite curves with a pair of compasses, a coin or something else round, above and below your depth line as shown. The radius of the 'lower' curve will be a slightly smaller arc. Notice how you also position this curve to meet the bottom edge at the end of your block. The convex curve will be at the top of your completed carving when it is standing up. The concave curve wants to be about a third up from the bottom of your standing figure, so as to leave a good, strong base below. Draw a line at right angles across the top side of your block from where the latter curve meets it, to join with your original, top side centre-line.

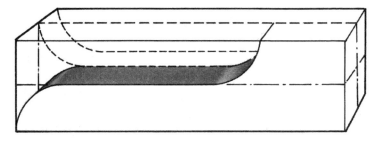

Fig. 61. Marking out for abstract figure.

I began carving with the convex curve end in mind and taking off plaster in layers as indicated by Fig. 62. All my chiselling was in the direction of the convex end but starting each layer progressively farther back towards what would eventually become the concave curve. When my layering reached down as far as the start of the convex curve, I began to develop it in small increments, cut by cut. Meanwhile, as I also got nearer to the concave end, I began to develop this curve, too, only a fraction at a time with each cut.

There is an important principle here. *Chiselling should always be directed away from a curve* – even though you are working back towards it. If you chisel, instead, towards a

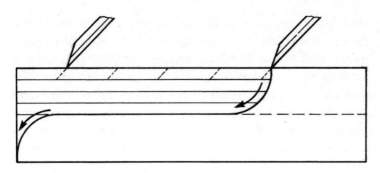

Fig. 62. Chisel cuts for abstract.

curve, you are likely to slip, take off more than you want, and ruin the curve. The best technique, unless you are unavoidably restricted, is always to chisel away from any delicate work, taking off no more than a 'whisker' with each cut. So, in all carving, somewhat paradoxically, it is usually better to work backwards whilst cutting forwards. This is particularly true when working in wood, because of the risk that the grain will 'run away' with the chisel. By working back but only chiselling forward, it then does not normally matter if the chisel slips and takes off more than is required. It follows that you may often have to vary the direction in which you chisel, to suit specific circumstances. You will learn when to invoke the above principle, mainly from practice and experience.

As shown in Fig. 62, start to chisel each layer at quite a steep angle but, as you proceed, lower this to about 15–20° as you cut away along the layer, keeping the bevel of the chisel tip uppermost. (Later, as you begin to increase the concave curve, you may find it an advantage to turn the chisel upside down to help negotiate the bend.)

If, as you begin, layer by layer, to remove material, the nearest edge of the block tares away a little, chamfer this edge and then work on down to it. Keep repeating this. Once you have established a reasonable depth across to the centre-line you can begin to use the developing inside wall of the block as its own guide for your chisel until this reaches down to the desired internal right angle.

When you reach the prescribed depth and your chiselled surface, including both curves, all looks 'deep and crisp and even', turn your block over. Mark out and work the other side similarly but with the curves in the opposite corners facing in the reverse direction to those on the first side.

When both sides are virtually identical – but reversed – your model is finished. I think you will see that the chisel-cut surface can scarcely be improved upon by using sand-paper, except perhaps to remove any remaining pencil marks. If, however, you feel you could further improve the surface of the curves, use the finest 'garnet' sandpaper. Wrap a piece of it around a dowel stick to work on the concave surface. (Garnet paper is the finest grade of abrasive paper, used mostly by jewellers.)

When I began carving this figure I used a retaining board but I finished off the work with it held on a sand bag so that I could vary the angle I was working for the curves. Although this piece was created purely as an exercise for this book, it has been greatly admired. I think the simplicity of form is quite appealing. (I now think this would look very good as a large 'monolith' in a wide open space.)

The finish for a sculpture like this is a matter of taste. I left mine just as it was carved, which I quite like but you may care to give yours a coat of emulsion paint. You could also introduce a contrasting colour for each side, which would be quite dramatic.

I like sculpture to be tactile and handled. However, if you leave such a piece as it is, or even if you put on colours, it may show finger-marks after being handled. A couple of coats of a clear, spray fixative will solve this problem. There are many spray fixatives available but they are all much of a muchness and I would probably use any that I happen to have at hand. However, if I were to buy one specially for this sort of carving, I would choose one of a sort suitable for charcoal or pastels.

Having started with the above simple but effective figure, I suggest you now design your own piece for carving. Keep it simple, graceful and not too difficult to carve. Let your imagination run freely. (You may find, as I do, that it is more difficult to design an abstract work than you first thought!)

More Advanced Carving

Now I suggest two figures which, whilst more demanding, should present no great difficulties:

'Naxos' man

An Eskimo fisherman.

I have given only the minimum of instructions as you should, by now, be able to consider how to approach the work and solve the problems. Think carefully in advance before you begin, mark out your work where necessary and be prepared to be flexible. Frequently, my work does not finish up as I intended when I started. I quite like this because: (a) it provides for spontaneity; (b) the material I am working on often dictates what I can and cannot do; and (c) it enables changes to be made when things go wrong. (Once, when working on a figure of a mother holding a child, in marble, the child's head fell off! I wasn't very pleased at the time but, subsequently, I was able to reposition and change the size of the child and thereby achieve a result which, I thought, after all, improved the figure.) So, don't worry when things go wrong or you make mistakes. You may have to put the carving aside for a while but continue to think about it and figure out what can be done to recover the work.

Naxos Man

Naxos man in Fig. 63 appeals because the figure is so simple; yet, so much can be learned from it. This is a figure which was found on the Greek Island of Naxos, and dates back to the sixth century BC.

Fig. 63. Naxos man.

The first thing to notice about this figure is how 'finished' it looks although far from completed. It conforms with the sound principle I first mentioned in Chapter 7: *a work of art should always be finished but never completed*. With the Naxos man, no part looks more worked on than any other part. The sculptor kept it all going at the same time, without concentrating on any one part until the whole figure was well formed and 'under control'. Because of this, it has a 'completed' look about it whilst, at the same time, leaving much of the 'reality' of its subject to your imagination. Notice how the genitals have been left in one solid mass with no attempt at refinement, and how the sculptor kept the arms in contact with the body, presumably both to simplify matters and to avoid the danger of them getting broken off.

The finish appears to be 'pot marked'. This is evidence of working with a pointed sculptor's tool held at right angles to the stone, the most common technique used, even today, for preliminary work on stone. This technique is unsuitable for plaster. You cannot achieve quite this same effect unless you work the figure all over with tiny punch marks.

I suggest you cast a block of plaster about 12 inches (30cm) tall and 6 inches (15cm) square. You want to have plenty of material to work on and remove. Start by marking out the centre-line; then outline the front, back and sides of the figure, ensuring that these all line up as they should.

Work to your outline marks, carving out a rough, overall shape as your first objective. You can begin by removing all the material *well outside* that overall shape but leaving plenty for finer shaping later. Use the saw where you can to remove large pieces, such as around the head.

When you come to the final shaping you can use a chisel or a rasp – which would leave a nice rough finish – or a combination of the two. Whether using chisel or rasp always remember the importance of driving your carving tool *out*-wards, away from curves whilst you work back towards them.

There is no reason why you should not develop your version of Naxos man further. Define the outlines of the neck, face and arms a little more but do not get carried away; still aim to leave a fairly rough impression. You could, if you wish, make a female figure by developing small breasts, a delicate pubis and slightly enlarged hips. You should be able to stop at any time once the human shape is evident, or carry on with the figure as far as you like. I find this figure very attractive and interesting.

Naxos man, being quite straightforward, is ideal for carving in any other material you might like to consider. You may wish to try Aircrete. This material is obtained from builders' yards. It is easy to work and often recommended as a starting material for students of sculpture. Aircrete is made up from various aggregate materials bound together with cement. It is a low in weight, rather gritty, makes more mess and it will blunt tools more. However, if you do decide to work with this material it is a good step towards working with stone. Against it, perhaps, is that it is quite unsuitable for working indoors – although a garage will do – and you need to switch from wood to masonry chisels. I also strongly recommend using a dust mask, overalls, goggles and protective gloves.

Eskimo Fisherman

This Eskimo, in Fig. 64, is one of the most delightful pieces of sculpture I have ever seen. It was in the exhibition of Eskimo (Inuit) sculpture held in London in the early 1970s. As a piece of sculpture, for me, it nears perfection. It is uncomplicated, graceful and perfectly captures the spirit of the subject. Only about 3½ inches (9cm) high it was carved in ivory – no doubt the tusk of a seal or sea lion – by an Eskimo, probably using only a knife.

For our purpose – and material – I suggest enlarging this figure quite considerably from the original. It will still retain much of its charm. A figure about 10 inches (25cm) high would be suitable.

Start with a rectangular, plaster block about 12 x 5 x 5 inches (30 x 12 x 12cm) and, as before, mark out the

Fig. 64. Eskimo.

centre-line and draw a rough outline of the figure on all sides of your block. Make a mark where the legs join together on the centre-line. This is lower than the crutch, which is hidden behind the overlapping anorak. Do not attempt a precise drawing; this outline is only a guide to your carving.

Now start to pare off the corners of the block. You can use a rasp for this, working vertically. Leave enough material in place for the arms, head and back-pack. Do not attempt any detail or 'finish' until you have completed the whole shape which should remain quite basic at this stage. You will notice some fish sticking out of his back-pack. I think these are quite charming and suitable for ivory but I recommend you to omit these, as they will, almost certainly, get broken off. (If you do not want the basket to look empty, you could make the top rounded as if packed with clothes.) Notice how the body leans slightly forward to counter-balance the pack – this demonstrates the perception and skill of the sculptor, no matter how untrained, and gives the figure its vitality. You need to develop this dynamic stance as you proceed. When you have a figure more or less of the right size and proportions, you can begin to pare away, very gently, towards the final shapes. Start the legs with a single, vertical saw cut and then continue to refine their forms with a chisel, rasp or knife. Make sure you leave very stubby legs with firm, strong feet to stand on. If you have got the balance correct, the figure should stand up well without support. Carved from plaster your Eskimo can be given a polished finish by buffing it up with white furniture polish.

Working from a 'Life' Figure

The suggestions which follow were specially posed for this book to provide simple, uncomplicated figures to be carved from cast plaster.

Fig. 65. Sennefer.

Sitting Figure

The idea for the first pose was prompted by the statue of Sennefer in the British Museum. The photograph in Fig. 65 shows Sennefer as being very compact and graceful. Carved from a cube-shaped block, a minimum amount of stone is removed. The arms and legs are only suggested by relief carving but one hand is raised above the main mass.

You may care to make a copy of Sennefer. However, I have also interpreted him, posed instead by a girl in a modern, draped version for you, in Fig. 66. I included the drapes here because these both look and lend themselves to sculpturing very well. They also eliminate detail and simplify the carving. I asked my model to rest her head forward as, in plaster, this is then much less vulnerable to getting broken off.

This figure should not present any undue difficulties if you proceed with care. Start with a large block of plaster. I suggest one 10 inches long x 10 inches tall x 8 inches wide (25 x 25 x 20cm). This is a fair-sized lump and you may have to make a box specially for casting it. On the other hand, you could carve a smaller copy, say, with all measures half or three-quarters of that size. (Make sure, whatever you decide, that your block is quite dry throughout before starting work.)

Mark out centre-lines along the front, top, back and, in this instance, also on each side and across the top. Roughly draw the appropriate outline of this girl on each visible face of your block, including the top. Make sure her figure is evenly distributed either side of the centre-lines without being too geometric.

Remove as much material as you can with a saw or by rough carving with a chisel. When you have this approximately hewn figure, you can move on to roughing out the final form. When that is done, begin working towards the finish. Keep everything in large masses. Make the drapes

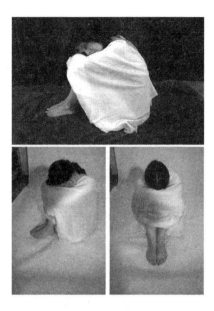

Fig. 66. Sitting girl with drapes.

sweep down towards the rear in lovely, undulating folds and identify the shapes of the arms supporting them. Develop the front of her legs and feet but do not carve out behind them; leave this filled in. Shape her head gracefully. You can choose mostly to hide her face, as in the lower pictures in Fig. 66, or you could try forming it in very simple outline, based on her holding her head on one side as in the top picture.

As always, it is vital to stop before you might overdo your work. Endeavour to make a firm decision on this as you attend to final touches. If you buff up with white, furniture polish to finish she should grace anywhere you choose to put her on display.

Crouched Figure

It would be very helpful if you can find someone to pose in this position for you. You will then discover more about the subject and shapes than may be possible from my descriptions and pictures here, in Figs. 67 and 68. In any event, study your subject carefully before you get started.

Start off as follows. Take a rectangular block of plaster. My block was an 8 x 5 inch rectangle, 6 inches deep (20 x 12 x 15cm) – but size is not critical. Mark out a centre-line along the top, continuing this down at each end. Draw an outline of the girl on the top, and on both sides. I have sketched these in Fig. 68 to help.

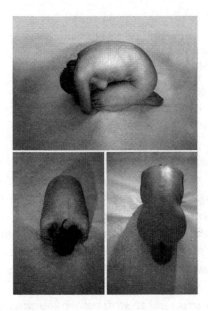

Fig. 67. Crouched girl.

I advise including a plinth in this figure. This will protect the feet which protrude from the body at the rear. So, score or mark out a plinth, before you start, around the bottom edges of the sides and the ends. About half an inch (1.25cm) thick will be sufficient.

Next remove the corners of the block by saw cuts, cutting vertically, down only as far as the plinth. Looking at Fig. 68, the heavier dotted lines of the lower diagram show where to cut. After cutting, a gentle tap sideways, with a chisel, should split free the unwanted material. Do not worry if the revealed surface remains a little rough. In the upper diagram of Fig. 68 you will see two more, quite large, triangular pieces, marked by heavy dotted lines which can also be removed by sawing, and one small triangular area (forward of and below the head), which can be sawn down and then chiselled out, or vice versa.

Now identify the highest point, which is at the top of her arched back, and the widest part, which will be her hips.

Develop these two areas first. As emphasised earlier, your chiselling direction needs to be outward, away from each of these target areas.

Keep your carving pretty rugged at this stage. Notice, as you begin work on lower features, that the folded legs extend wider than the body at the waist but remain a little narrower than the hips where they join those. You must shape all of this very carefully, keeping the masses quite solid and ample for the moment. It is all too easy to work too quickly and remove too much. Similarly, with the head and arms, just leave roughly cut block, with no attempt at detail as yet. Take care to leave material for the feet and that, depending exactly how your model has placed her hands (see Fig. 67), you have also allowed sufficient block out of which to carve them later. When you have a good overall figure with the right proportions and everything in the right place, take a well-earned break.

After that, start refining and working towards the finish. *DON'T OVERDO IT*. Fine detail is very difficult in plaster

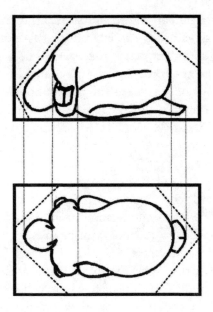

Fig. 68. Saw cuts.

and you may easily spoil the end result. Most of the areas are quite straightforward and you should not have too much difficulty in working with your chisel. However, there is one area where you may find your ordinary, flat chisel is not so useful. This is the area between the legs and the waist. Here you may have to work, instead, carefully, with a knife. However, I am tempted to suggest you buy a very cheap set of wood-carving tools. *Do not buy good quality tools* for this work. The sort I have in mind are sold in sets, like the one shown in Fig. 69, in a plastic holder. You see them on market stalls and in DIY shops. They are really quite unsuitable for wood carving as they are made from cheap, carbon steel which breaks very easily and cannot be re-sharpened. **I would never use high quality, and expensive, wood carving tools on plaster.** Whereas, I often use these cheap tools. When you buy them they are very sharp, so do be careful of the cutting edge. Tap with a mallet rather than drive them by hand. You will find the curved gauges quite useful for getting into awkward places such as this area you are now working on.

Fig. 69. Inexpensive set of carving tools.

To carve detail into the hands resting on the arms or the leg, you will have to be very careful indeed or you will easily chop them off. First, cut a V-shape groove around where they rest, and then chisel away from them – NOT towards them. Work similarly with the feet. Carve as much as you can in a horizontal direction, AWAY from them, and be very careful indeed as you finish off. Use any 'tool' you can lay your hands on, if necessary. The ends of a nail file can be used to scrape away plaster, little by little; or sandpaper, wrapped around, say, a kebab stick sharpened into a point, can be used to remove material. With plaster, you can scrape as well as cut and carve. The main thing is to get the result and not damage the work.

Warning! You may find that the last touch you are tempted to do – for perfection – will spoil the whole thing. Resist the temptation!

When you have reached this degree of satisfaction you should stop.

I would tend to leave this figure white, buffed up only with white furniture polish. If you would like to create a contrast with the plinth, you could colour that before applying the polish. I think a black mount would make too severe a contrast and suggest a chestnut colour. Other finishes and colourings from which you can choose are all to be found at the end of Chapter 4.

Well, that completes this book but I hope for many it really will be just the beginning. Practice makes perfect and practical experience is much more valuable than written instruction. Practise as much, and as often, as you can. Do so to gain experience rather than for exhibition. Remember, all great professionals, whatever their calling, practise alone for hours each day.

Glossary

Abstract	Work which is unlike any other known subject.
'Aircrete'	Lightweight building blocks made from various aggregate materials bound together with cement.
Armature	Internal support for modelling.
Armature wire	Flexible wire to support clay on an armature.
Assemblage	Work employing the use of various materials. (See Constructions.)
Bronzing	Applying colour to produce a bronze-like effect.
Bust peg	Main support for modelling a head.
Butterfly	Two pieces of wood or similar material, set crossways, to support clay.
Callipers	A pair of compass arms for measuring distances between points.
Carving	Removing material to create work.
Chipping	Removing plaster from a waste mould.
Clay	A malleable sedimentary material which occurs naturally.
Constructions	Three-dimensional sculpture made from various materials.

Cyanoacrylate	'Superglue'.
File	A sharp-toothed tool for removing material.
Firing	Baking clay in a kiln oven.
Fixatives	Substances applied over art work to prevent smudging or finger marks.
Glaze	A vitreous coating applied to give an impervious surface or for decoration.
Grog	Ground-up fired clay mixed with unfired clay to give texture and strength.
Intaglio	Relief work cut below the surface.
Keys	Indentures made to locate exactly one part of a multiple mould to another.
Kiln	A specially constructed oven for baking (firing) clay.
Leather hard	Clay before it has fully dried out.
Maquette	A small example made as a model for a larger work.
MDF	Medium-density fibreboard used in building, model making and art work.
Minimalism	A work reduced to the minimum amount of detail.
Modelling	Manipulating a malleable material to produce work.
Modelling stand	A support for work whilst modelling. Often a turntable, adjustable for height.
Moulds	A negative image from which a positive is cast.
Patination	The surface colourings added mainly to metal sculpture to obtain a desired effect.
Plaster	A white powder made from gypsum which sets hard when mixed with water.

Plasticine	A plastic material, made from clay and oils, used for modelling.
Pottery	Vessels and artefacts made from fired clay.
Rasp	A coarse-toothed file for removing material.
Release agent	Substance applied to the internal surface of moulds to enable them to be parted easily from casts made therein.
Relief	Sculpture which stands out from, or is cut into, a flat surface.
Rifflers	Curved files for removing material.
Sand box	Tray of sand for holding figure whilst working.
'Scratch and dab'	Scratching surfaces which are to be joined and moistening them with water.
Sculpture	Works of art made in three dimensions.
Shellac	A resin which is made into a varnish.
Shim	A piece of fencing, usually metal, used to make a partition or division between parts of a mould.
Stylised	A work which is not an exact copy of an original but which suggests its particular style.
Turntable	A rotating platform upon which to work.
Undercuts	Recesses below an overhanging surface.
Wax	A sticky plastic material used for modelling and casting.
Wedging	'Kneading' clay to remove pockets of air and excess moisture.
Wetting down	Applying moisture to clay to keep it workable.

Appendix

Suppliers of Tools and Materials

Artists' colour powders and shellac:
L Cornelissen & Son Ltd
105 Great Russell Street
London WC1B 3RY
Tel: 020 7636 1045
www.cornelissen.com

Clay:
Potclays Ltd
Brickkiln Lane
Etruria
Stoke on Trent ST4 7BP
Tel: 01782 219816
www.potclays.co.uk

'Wimbourne' table easel and artists' materials:
Daler-Rowney Ltd – and good art shops
Peacock Lane
Bracknell
Berkshire RG12 8ST
Tel: 01344 424621
www.daler-rowney.com

Sculpture suppliers, tools, materials and books:
Shop/mail order:
Alec Tiranti Ltd
70 High Street
Theale
Reading, Berkshire RG7 5AR
Tel: 0118 930 2775

Shop:
Alec Tiranti Ltd
27 Warren Street
London W1T 5NB
Tel: 020 7636 8565
www.tiranti.co.uk

Modelling wax:
Poth Hille & Co Ltd
37 High Street
Stratford
London E15 2QD
Tel: 020 8534 7091
www.poth-hille.co.uk

Stone and marble mounts:
Nigel Owen, Stoneworkers
42 High Street
Yelvertoft
Northampton NN6 6LQ
Tel: 01788 822281

Index